You Are God

You Are God

Mark Clinton Patterson BA, Cht.

Writers Club Press
San Jose New York Lincoln Shanghai

You Are God

All Rights Reserved © 2000 by Mark Clinton Patterson

No part of this book may be reproduced or transmitted in any form or by any means, graphic, electronic, or mechanical, including photocopying, recording, taping, or by any information storage retrieval system, without the permission in writing from the publisher.

Writers Club Press
an imprint of iUniverse.com, Inc.

For information address:
iUniverse.com, Inc.
620 North 48th Street, Suite 201
Lincoln, NE 68504-3467
www.iuniverse.com

Disclaimer: Throughout this book, statements are made pertaining to the properties and/or functions of nutritional products. These statements have not been evaluated by the Food and Drug Administration and these materials and products are not intended to diagnose, treat, cure or prevent any disease.

ISBN: 0-595-13449-1

Printed in the United States of America

Dedication

This book is dedicated to Betty Ann Jiron the love of my life, Spiritual Partner and Soulmate. You are my inspiration, guidance, and wisdom.

Contents

Chapter One
What Happens When We Die? 1

Chapter Two
Seeing God Everywhere 8

Chapter Three
Messages From the Masters 27

Chapter four
Religion's Dark Side 38

Chapter Five
Knowing the Matrix of God 44

Chapter Six
The Matrix of Your Dreams 54

Chapter Seven
The Matrix of Sexuality 60

Chapter Eight
The Imprint of HIV/AIDS 66

Chapter Nine
Healing the Matrix of Sexuality 79

viii • You Are God

Chapter Ten
The Matrix of the Gift Behind All Things 90

Chapter Eleven
The Imprint of Violence 94

Chapter Twelve
Healing the Matrix of Race 97

Chapter Thirteen
Healing the Matrix of Gender 101

Chapter Fourteen
The Matrix of Dr. Deeper 103

Chapter Fifteen
The Matrix of Las Cruces, New Mexico 109

Chapter Sixteen
The Matrix of Sound 111

Chapter Seventeen
The Matrix of the Imagination 113

Chapter Eighteen
The Matrix of the Possible Human 115

Chapter Nineteen
The Matrix of the Future 117

Preface

The word's that are contained within the pages of this book are my words. This is my story based on my Near Death Experience on February 1st, 1986. I ask that you do not believe them. I ask that you go within the depths of your being and decide if they are true for you. If they resonate within you, then we share a common truth. If it does not, then it becomes my truth. Because of my profound experience 14 years ago, I realize that I am no different from the homeless, the beggar, the thief, the derelict, or the person with AIDS. At any given moment I am one decision away from becoming any one of them. I also know that at any given moment I am one decision away from remembering my intimate connection to God, the Divine that is within. It is my hope and intention that this book will lead all life everywhere to remember that intimate connection to God. Namaste!

Acknowledgements

There are so many people to thank. To those of you who have come into my life, and mine into yours I hope that we have seen the truth of our relationship. We were brought together so that we could learn from each other. No matter how painful that lesson may have felt at the time, each and everyone of you who has blessed my life, came into it, to show me all aspects of my self. Thank you for being my greatest teachers. Thank you for reflecting back too me my shadow self. Without you, this book would not be possible. I love you and honor you!

List of Contributors

A special thanks to Cythina Roberts for editing the ramblings of my eccentric mind. Thanks to Dr. Kelley Elkins, Toni Delgado, and Dr. Dean Jacob's for their unconditional compassion, love, and support while writing this book. Thanks to Dr. Doreen Virtue, Ken Page, Lee Caroll, Drunvalo Melchizedek, Gregg Braden, Dick and Tara Sutphen, Barbara Ann Brennan, Dr. Deepak Chopra, Marianne Willamson, and Neale Donald Walsch for their permission to quote and or their influence in my life.

Chapter One

What Happens When We Die?

On February 1, 1986, I had a Near Death Experience (NDE). I was an irrational teenager who thought it would be really cool to consume vast amounts of alcohol. After two beers, four wine coolers and a fifth of vodka, my body went into cardiac arrest and I found myself in Heaven. Twenty-two minutes later, another soul came in and took the place of the original. In other words, I am a walk-in. However, something very unusual happened—the soul that took over after the original one left walked in from the future. Former NASA Physicist Barbara Ann Brennan writes in Hands of Light: "Future lifetimes can be placed in the auric field at birth and can be taken on at the completion of a lifetime if the individual so chooses." (Brennan, p. 262)

So, basically I reincarnated into the same body. I evolved five lifetimes with a fifth of vodka. (Please do not try this at home, as you may not get the same results as I did.) As I lay unconscious on the bathroom floor of the Canterbury Suite in Coralville, Iowa, I began to hear an incredibly beautiful sound—a sound so healing that it was, and is, beyond description. My attention then switched to the fact that I was no longer in my body. I panicked. I called out to my classmates, who just an hour earlier were chanting "go, go, go" as I was chugging down a fifth of vodka. But my cries for help fell upon deaf ears. No one could see that I was dead; no one could see that I was no longer in my body. What was most terrifying was the fact that no one could hear me. The music from the celestial choir filled me with an overwhelming feeling of peace and love. My "vision" looked upward and I saw the gates of Heaven open before my eyes. there was an iridescent glowing light. It was as if I was being pulled by a magnetic force into the light. I was at complete peace—there was no pain, no sadness, just love.

I was then greeted by five angels. They must have been 10 to 12 feet in height and they glowed with a bluish-white color. An absolute love radiated from them to me. They took me to a room with a table; the table was transparent and looked like a hologram. They proceeded to say, "This is your life." The table then turned into images of the life I had been living, and the dialogue between my angels and me went something like this:

Mark: "My father left me when I was three. He is pathetic; I hate him."

Angels: "How does that relate to love?"

Mark: "My mother, she is never around and never listens to me. I hate her, too."

Angels: "How does that relate to love?"

Mark: "There is my cousin, Shawn. Watch me kick his ass."

Angels: "How does that relate to love?"

Mark: "My neighbor is black. I don't like black people."

Angels: "How does that relate to love?"

Mark: "You see John over there? He is gay, a fucking faggot, homosexual."

Angels: "How does that relate to love?"

Mark: "Look at all of my classmates. They suck, fuck them all."

Angels: "How does that relate to love?"

Mark: "There is that TV evangelist telling me that I need to be saved. Fuck that Jesus shit."

Angels: "How does that relate to love?"

Mark: "Oh, you keep saying that. How does what relate to love?"

Angels: "Mark, everything in life is a test to see if you will respond with fear or love. You are not being judged here. However, there is one thing that you will be measured by—your ability to love unconditionally. When you learn to respond only with love, then you will evolve and thus end the cycle of karma and reincarnation.

"Jesus was sent to Earth to show people how to end the cycle of karma and reincarnation. This is done through compassion, forgiveness, and non-judgment. When you respond with hate, blame, fear and resentment, you create the same experiences over and over again, lifetime after lifetime. Eventually, you become what you most hate. Throughout your lifetimes, you will experience various roles—good, bad, rich, poor, victim and martyr. As you experience all things, you will realize there is nothing and no one to judge. When you let go of judgment, you will develop compassion for all life. Once you do that, the cycle of karma and reincarnation will end. By the looks of things, you are going to incarnate as a black, gay, overweight, TV evangelist in your next lifetime. Karma was never intended to be a punishment. It was given to humanity to ensure that each and every one of you would be held 100 percent responsible for your own life. That is why Jesus said, 'Do unto others as you would have them do unto to you.'"

Mark: "Lifetime after lifetime? I am going to come back as an overweight, gay, black male who preaches about Jesus? Wait a minute? How does that relate to love?"

Angels: "Yes, lifetime after lifetime. You call it reincarnation. You see, Mark, you chose the parents that you hate before you came here. You made agreements and contract with them before you incarnated on Earth. Everything is already laid out for you. All things are predestined. The only thing you can control is how you respond to what happens to you. You chose a pattern that was set in the stars at the time of your conception, a path that would most help you evolve."

Doreen Virtue, Ph.D., writes the following in *The Light Workers Way*:

> Before your birth, you and a spiritual council of guides created a life plan tailored to meet your material, spiritual, and karmic needs. This

Divine plan has three elements: a purpose, personal growth lessons, and relationships with other people to support the overall plan.

Your purpose is a task you are to do through your career, volunteer work, or a special project that uses your natural talents and interests to benefit humanity. Your plan's second element entails well-timed life events that teach you about love and help you to shed self-defeating personality traits.

The third element involves pre-birth arrangements you made with certain people who will serve as catalysts for your purpose and personal growth. These people may function as your family members, co-workers, friends, or acquaintances. Your interactions with these people simultaneously help them to fulfill their own plans.

Your predestined plan is a rough outline of what your life would look like, including your purpose, significant life lessons, and relationships with particular people. Because the plan is only a rough outline, you must choose the finer details of your plan as you go through life. You are free to ignore the plan completely but the emotional and societal consequences of this choice can be devastating. (Virtue, p. 72)

Of course, you have forgotten all of this. The areas in life that you most struggle with are those where you have not yet learned self-mastery. You have forgotten to remember your natural state of love. Instead of demonstrating your self-mastery, you have demonstrated your fears.

Don't worry, you will have unlimited opportunities to demonstrate love. Love is what makes all things possible. Love is the answer. Love is who you are, be that love."

Then the angels introduced me to a brilliant being. He had to be 20 feet tall and I felt an incredible love coming from him to me. The angels explained that I was going to go home to God now and that this being would take over for me and complete the rest of my physical life. They said that they would always be in my heart and not to forget them, that they loved me and that I was never alone. At that moment, my consciousness shifted from walking into a pristine place of peace to this brilliant being who was about to enter my body. In one breath, I was literally "slammed" into a completely unconscious body. The amount of energy that it takes to awaken a "dead" body is phenomenal. It was as if I had been struck by lightning.

My face lay in a pool of blood and vomit. My body and face had turned completely green. I could not breathe and passed out once again. Several hours later, my friends drove me home, as my mom was gone for the weekend. When I woke up, it was as if I had never been on Earth before. I felt very frightened, but then recalled who spoke to me while I was passed out the previous night. Merlin had visited me in my drunken state of oblivion and revealed a caste system that was the hierarchy of the Alpha and Omega Order of Melchizedek. (Yes, Merlin as in Arthur and the Knights of the Round Table.). He explained my relationship to this hierarchy. Did Merlin really come to me that night? Did he really describe the geometric caste system of the Melchizedek priesthood? Yes, I am now convinced of it. But for now, I want to go back to the question that I was asked by my angels during my Near Death Experience: "How does that relate to love?"

I find it funny, this "What would Jesus do?" Really, what would Jesus do? Do you really think that if Jesus was here, he would be out on corners asking people, "Are you saved?" Or telling them, "You need to be saved!" Do you think he would say, "AIDS is God's way of punishing those for being gay?" Or that he would condemn people for being gay or lesbian? Do you think he would condemn people who choose to be in an interracial marriage? Do you think he would suppress women as the Catholic Church has done? Would Jesus condone the Catholic Church's response to most wife beatings? Or divorce requests? Do you think that he would be pleased to see what the Catholic Church has done with his teachings? Do you think that he would be pleased to see the wealth of the Vatican and the majority of churches, and the poverty of their followers? Or that he would be pleased to see the TV Evangelist who says, "God has a message for you—send in those checks now!" Do you think that he would call Jews sinners who need to be converted? Do you think he would call upon the Islamic Fundamentalist to be saved? Do you really think that he would call anyone a sinner? Indeed, What would Jesus do? The question is not, "What would Jesus do?" The real question is, "What would love do?"

When you are lying on your death bed, you will not worry about the money, cars, or homes that you collected on the way. You will wonder about the relationship with your father that you did not heal. You will wonder about your spouse and remember how you refused to forgive him or her for what was done to you so many years ago. You will wonder if you loved your children enough. You will ask, "Why was I so angry?" You will wonder about the relationship with your children that you did not heal. You will cry over the person to whom you forgot to say, "I love you." You will be measured by one thing, and one thing only, while here on Earth. That is love. So, the next time you are angry, in pain, in resentment, filled with blame and rage, stop and ask yourself, "How does this relate to love?" If you knew that you only had one hour to live and you knew who you would call and what you would say…If you already know, then what are you waiting for?

I find it strange that people who say you need to be saved from the depths of Hell base their judgements on something they have never experienced. Hell was a village outside of Jerusalem where people burned their garbage. It was always burning, smouldering, and was filled with smoke and the stench of garbage. Jesus used the word "Hell" as a metaphor. You are not going to go to Hell when you die, no matter what you do or don't do. It is impossible. It is impossible for you NOT to get to God. Thus, all roads lead to God. Some roads are more direct, effortless, and fun! Other roads are bumpy, but regardless of which road you choose, you will always get to God.

Does this mean that you should do whatever you want without care or concern about possible consequences? NO! Everything that you think, say, and do—as well as the motive behind everything you think say and do—creates karma. There is no right or wrong, just outcomes for everything that you think, say, and do. "As you sow, so shall you reap." If you are filled with fear, anger, blame, and resentment, your life will be Hell on Earth. On the other hand, if you evolve and learn to express unconditional love, you will experience Heaven on Earth. Your mind can choose to tune into the matrix of Hell or the matrix of Heaven. There are only two matrixes—a matrix of Love and the matrix of Fear.

Chapter Two

Seeing God Everywhere

What if God is not some "male" being sitting on his throne in Heaven, casting his judgments upon everything you do while dictating every moment of your life? (One of the Judeo-Christian names for God is "Elshadi," which translates into "the breasted one." But if this is true, then this of course would imply that God was/is a female. The Catholic Church couldn't have that, now could they?) What if God is not a male who is waiting for you to die so that you can plead with him to let you into Heaven? What if God is not a male who will throw mercy on your soul, saving you from eternal damnation? Rather, what if God is a matrix that is woven into all life, everywhere—in ALL things?

To the writers, directors, and producers of the movie, "The Matrix," I cannot thank you enough. Whether it was metaphoric, intentional, unintentional, or by random chance, you have explained the truth about this reality in a remarkable way. A matrix is reality, and you can tune into whatever reality, or matrix, you wish. The one you tune into is largely based on the decisions, events, and experiences you hold in your "auric" field from the moment of conception to the time of physical death. (The auric field is the electromagnetic field that surrounds the physical body.) However, there are also "imprints" or other matrixes in your auric field that were created in other lifetimes.

Your auric field senses and perceives things before you do. It also acts as a magnet in the sense that your thoughts become an instruction guide for the auric field. Once your auric field is filled with enough like thoughts or imprints, it will create and attract into your life that which reflects those thoughts and imprints back to you. Thus, the idea: "Change your thinking, change your life."

If you have a matrix that surrounds you, and if the matrix of God is woven through all things, then it becomes very natural for us to see God everywhere. The more we think in terms of reality as a matrix, it becomes increasingly impossible for us not to see God. It becomes impossible for us not to see all life as interwoven and interconnected. It becomes impossible for us not to see the ONENESS of all life, everywhere. It becomes impossible for us not to become One with God. As we tune into the matrix of God, we let go of fear and become the matrix of love. We become God. Again, there is only the matrix of love and the matrix of fear. But in order for us to tune into the matrix of God, we must heal our own matrix and imprints of fear. I believe that we as a race make the following decisions about ourselves, which create imprints deep in our own matrix (or auric field). These keep us trapped in the matrix of fear and stuck in the cycle of karma and reincarnation. Often, traumatic events from previous lifetimes lead us to these decisions. (Later in this chapter, I will explain how this relates to previous lifetimes and illness.)

- I am a victim.
- I am not wanted.
- I am unworthy.
- No matter what I do, it won't make a difference anyway.
- I am not understood.
- I am powerless, hopeless, and helpless.
- I am not safe here on Earth.
- I am unable to protect myself.
- If I fully give of myself, I will get hurt or betrayed.
- It is not safe for me to love.

- I cannot trust anyone.
- It is not safe for me to feel.
- It is not safe for me to express my feelings.
- I am not enough.
- I didn't do enough.
- I am not capable.
- I cannot handle it.
- I am being punished.
- I have been left all alone and am lonely.
- I need another to make me complete.
- I am guilty.
- I am unlovable.

Once these decisions have been made, they control our lives until we become clear of them. Are your wheels spinning in your mind? Once you start thinking in terms of reality as a matrix, then you can be open to miracles and you will see God in all people —including yourself—and in all things, everywhere.

Now, let's go back to these decisions and how they keep us stuck in the matrix of fear. Let's say that as a child you were sexually violated. This violation creates an imprint or matrix that says, "I am unable to protect me. I am guilty. I am bad. I am dirty." This imprint also has a biochemical component to it that remains in the body until it is released. No matter how hard you try to block this event from your memory, the matrix remains. Often, it is the woman who was sexually violated as a teen who gains weight to protect herself from being attractive. Her imprint is, "If I am beautiful, then I will be violated again." Energy never dies, it only transforms.

Therefore, these imprints act like magnets to shape our reality. You must realize that everyone and everything has a matrix around it. If your matrix is imprinted with the thought that "I am not enough," then your world will reflect that. Your auric field will continually draw experiences into your life that reflect "I am not enough." This is the law of attraction. Because there are plenty of people out there with the matrix that says, "I am better than others," you will attract these people into your life. Then you will measure and compare yourself to them, and in doing so, will get to be right about not being enough. Are you begining to see the implications of accepting life as a reflection of your matrix? Which matrix are you willing to tune into to?

What happens is that we attract people, places, and events that reflect back to us what is occurring in our own matrixes. Do you see how powerful you really are? All of it is a reflection of you. Thus, the world becomes your mirror; you can see all aspects of yourself, both light and dark. Many people want to learn from Jesus, Buddha, Sia Baba, or Mother Mary. Yet the person who can teach you the most is that no-good SOB that lives across the street. That person would not be in your life if it was not for the patterns or imprints in your matrix. This is karma. This is what you came here to resolve. I hear many people refer to their life as a mess because their Moon is in Cancer. When the stars were set into motion at your birth, you received the astrological imprint that will influence your entire life. It was given to you to transform. Unfortunately, for most of us, instead of transforming our Moon squaring in Pluto, we became stuck in the dark aspect of our astrological configuration. More often than not, our imprints keep us stuck in the past where, according to the law, we will create the same experiences over and over again, lifetime after lifetime.

This concept can also be applied to Vietnam veterans who suffer from post-traumatic war syndrome. Their matrix of reality has become so distorted that they have forgotten how to turn off the matrix and imprints of war. The war experience is stuck in their matrix and remains "on" all of the time. What we don't realize is that this matrix can be switched off. Likewise, we have switched the matrix of God off, but it is still there. It is in all things and in all people. We just need to turn it back on. This is just like a situation in which someone who could walk at one time becomes paralyzed due to an accident. The body remembers how to walk because the matrix of walking is still there and can never be taken away. The matrix of God has always been within you; it never left. So, what if the matrix of walking could simply be turned back on again? I believe that it can.

In his best-selling book, *Ageless Body Timeless Mind,* Deepak Chopra, M.D., tells an incredible story of how memories at the cellular level, if changed, can produce changes within a person's lifestyle. He tells of a woman who was to receive a heart from a younger male. Now, at no time prior to the heart transplant did she eat at McDonald's or drink beer. However, shortly after the heart transplant operation, she began to crave McDonald's food and beer. As it turned out, McDonald's and beer were the young man's favorite food. This implies that a matrix of awareness exists at the cellular level. If new information can be stored in this matrix of awareness, then physiological changes will result.

(Deepak Chopra, M.D., is an endocrinologist and is considered by many to be the pioneer in the field of alternative healing. His numerous best-selling books include *Ageless Body Timeless Mind* and *Quantum Healing.*)

Here is another example of how this works. Let's take a parrot. A parrot does not have a tongue, vocal chords, or physical brain capable of producing speech. Yet, how does it recognize and reproduce speech? What if the parrot has a matrix of awareness or a matrix of consciousness that connects into the matrix of speech? Or what if the parrot's matrix is simply connected to into the matrix of consciousness itself. This is similar to what Carl Jung meant with his idea of the collective unconscious. It is this interaction of the matrixes that enables a parrot to replicate speech without the necessary vocal chords.

Now, let's explore this idea of the matrix of consciousness a bit further. As we become aware of this matrix of God, we can clearly understand how the hundredth monkey phenomenon could happen. In the late 1960s, researchers were studying the behavior of monkeys in the Galapagos islands. They noticed that when a monkey ate a potato, it was a very messy process because the potato was covered in sand and dirt. One day, one of the monkeys washed the potato off with water before eating it. A domino effect then occurred. Like magic, all of the other monkeys on that island began to wash their potatoes before eating them. Then, monkeys on surrounding islands, who had never seen the first monkey wash a potato, simultaneously began to wash their potatoes. This implies that if enough beings of a race or species do something, then everyone else begins to replicate it. Once one person does something, it is placed into the matrix of consciousness so that anyone can do it. If Jesus can do it, anyone can do it. We are all one.

Now, think about the implications of this. It is simply mind blowing. What if healthy cells could communicate with diseased cells? What if the matrix for walking could simply be turned back on for a paralyzed person? What if the matrix of health could replace the imprint of disease and illness? What if the body could re-create itself? During the past few years, I have demonstrated that breast augmentation through hypnosis works! Lipid cells in the breast can be easily replicated in the body of a woman. I can increase a woman's bustline by two inches in as little as two hours! I have done this live, on the air, with before-and-after measurements taken by another woman! I am convinced that the body is designed to re-create and regenerate itself. Likewise, when you break a bone, the only thing that a cast does is set the bone in place. Your body does the rest—new cells, new connective tissue, new bone masses. It re-creates itself and you end up with a bone that is no longer broken. Your cells are in constant replication. The following excerpt is taken from. Keith D. Clark's book, entitled *You Are Sharp Enough To Be Your Own Surgeon.*

The physical body that each of us possesses (or possesses us) is made up of roughly 50 trillion cells. About 30 billion of these are nerve cells. Everyday millions of cells throughout our bodies are being replaced. This takes place through the normal process of attrition and replacement. Indeed, 98% of our body is replaced within one year. The remaining cells are replaced the following year. In fact, 10% of all cells in your body are replaced every three weeks, 25% of the cells are replaced every 5-6 weeks. The cells that make up our skin are totally new every 30 days. The cells that make up the soft muscle tissue of our internal organs are replaced in two to three months. The liver is replaced within six weeks, while the stomach lining takes as little as four days. Some cells, such as those closely involved in the process of digestion, are replaced as rapidly as every five minutes! (Clark, p. 5)

You see that the matrix of regeneration and re-creation is always working in your body. You simply need to learn how to use this matrix to create healing. The pattern of perfect health is within your matrix of consciousness. Since your body is designed to re-create and regenerate itself, you just need to turn that matrix back on again. Here is an open letter from a Viet Nam Vet who took the time to discover how to turn the matrix of feeling and mobility
back on.

> My name is Wayne and this letter is being penned after spending 12 hours—over a period of 2 days—and receiving 12 treatments with Dr. Kelley Elkins I am 53 years old/young and I have been in chronic/severe pain for 34 of those years. Much of my physical pain can be traced back to my tour in Viet Nam, where I was a door gunner in a helicopter squadron.

> Like so many others, my chopper was shot down while on a mission. My injuries included a separated skull resulting in severe migraines; blurred vision; and low, dull ringing in my ears. I suffered a dislocated shoulder, knee, and a cracked knee cap, several cracked ribs, a collapsed lung, cracked jaw bone, broken leg, wrist and ankle, a deep bone hip bruise, broken nose, bruised kidneys, internal bleeding and a sundry of bruises and contusions. I was unconscious for 30 days,

received the Last Rites twice, and was basically given very little chance of surviving my many injuries.

However, my physical pain was nothing compared to the mental, emotional, psychological, and spiritual pain/crisis experienced. After my crash, I spent 16 months in various hospitals where doctors tried to piece me back together the best that they could through surgery and physical therapy. Unfortunately, only my physical ailments were addressed. I was labeled anti-social with suicidal tendencies. (Imagine that!) Once they deemed me well enough physically, I received a medical discharge. The physical pain was overwhelming and triggered the abuse of drugs and alcohol to the point of extinction.

Meanwhile my emotional and mental capacities were falling apart at the seams. I experienced flashbacks, deep-rooted shame, rage, fear, guilt, blame, suicidal thoughts, and a need to withdrawal from everyone. Ironically, the more that I tried to numb myself, the more severe the pain; flashbacks, deep-rooted shame, rage, fear, guilt, blame, suicidal thoughts, and alienation intensified. My abuses were nearly killing me.

Thankfully, all of my pain drove me to my knees. I experienced a total break down and then my real war began…Through God's Grace and Love, I finally realized that I dearly wanted to live, not exist, not merely survive in my numb, dumb, and dead "Blackness." With all of my heart and soul, I began the journey back to the light. Many hours, days, weeks, months and years were used up attempting to heal and grow. Many traditional methods were used and explored. After years of struggling, a new crisis arose. I ruptured a disc in my lower back which required surgery.

Due to the pain, I was given powerful medication and my downward spiral began anew. I fell deeper and deeper into my "Blackness." I went from one traditional treatment to the next, and nothing would relieve the pain. I lost my will to live. I was at a loss as to where to turn next. I finally got to the point where I didn't want to go on any longer, I just wanted to go into oblivion.

That is when I met Kelley Elkins. While what he was saying seemed, shall I say, strange, his gentleness, depth, and honesty intrigued me. So, I decided to try one last time to find release from my pain and self-imposed exile. On Saturday, March 27, 1999, I went to Kelley in hopes that he could assist me in my healing. Yes, I was eager to try. Yes, I was scared beyond belief. Yes, I had intense doubts and fears. Yet, what else was I to do? So, with high hopes, and deep fears, and many disbeliefs the treatment began.

The first thing that struck me was Kelley's insistence that he was only a facilitator and that I was the actual healer. All I needed to do was have faith in myself, the process, and that I could heal if I chose. This is due to the fact that I am a child of God and that God promises us we can have abundance, wholeness and unconditional love. The second thing that struck me was the gentleness of the procedure. The third things was his compassion and intuitiveness. Fourth, I experienced a feeling of energy due to the release of pain, followed by a sense of peace.

With each treatment, the pain diminished. It was replaced with a warmth that soon spread throughout my entire body. By the end of the second day, I knew that my hopes had not only been met but surpassed beyond my wildest imagination. I left Kelley a NEW PERSON. Not only was I pain free, there were other wonderful effects as well. The ringing in my ears was gone. The blurring haze has departed. My sense of smell increased. I felt a warmth vibrating deep within that feels life giving and healing. I feel alive and whole for the first time in many, many years, if not the first time in my life.

I would like to encourage anyone, especially if they are a Vietnam Vet, to make an appointment with Kelley and see what he has to offer. When all else has failed, what do you have to lose except your pain? It was a truly amazing healing experience of the Mind/Body/Soul…In conclusion, I would like to quote, Martin Luther King "Free at last, free at last, Thank you God, free from pain at last." I pray that you open yourself to this experience and that you find release, peace, and LOVE.

Wayne

You may visit Dr. Kelley Elkins at: *http://www.angelfire.com/nm/elkins-delgado* I encourage you to make an appointment if you need to free yourself from traumatic emotional imprints. I would also like to extend an invitation to Christopher Reeve to make an appointment with Dr. Elkins. The body remembers how to walk. In my opinion, Dr. Elkins has techniques which can turn that memory back on. "Superman," you have nothing to loose and everything to gain.

Here is another example of how these imprints influence our health. Let's say that as a child, your father abandoned you at the age of 5. As a child, you grew up measuring and comparing yourself to children who did have fathers. Thus, you developed a deep resentment around this issue; at an emotional level you were constantly longing for what might have been. This imprint created a pattern within your matrix that said, "People who love me will leave me, so it is not safe for me to love." In order to deal with this, you began to crave sugar. In fact you ate so much sugar that you developed diabetes. Have you noticed that whenever you are lonely and depressed, you begin to crave sugar? Now that you have this imprint of abandonment in your auric field, you will attract relationships that reflect this back to you. Thus, you will continue to consume sugar until you create serious health problems for yourself. Do you understand the cyclical nature of the matrix? Do you understand that emotional imprints are the underlying cause of "dis-ease"? The word "dis-ease" means just that—you are not at ease with yourself. Once you heal the imprint of abandonment, then you heal your resentment. Once you heal your resentment, you will have a new matrix that doesn't feed off of sugar. Again, matrixes feed into each other due to the law of attraction. Since the body re-creates itself, you will be healed of diabetes. This is how it works.

So, how do you turn the matrix of God back on? You must first begin to see the matrix of God in all things, people and events. As you see the matrix of God everywhere, then you will see the matrix of God that is within you, that is you. "When you see the Son in that Father, you will see the Father in the Son." When you see the Christ in other people, you will see the Christ in yourself. As you become aware of the matrix of God that is you, then all things in your life will be healed. If you are in need of a healing and you have been praying for one, STOP waiting for the voice of GOD to speak to you. The matrix of God can be very gentle and soft, but you must be willing to drop expectations as to what it is going to look like, feel like, or sound like. You must surrender to the unlimited ways that the matrix of God can work through you. For example, a friend might say to you, "You know, I just saw the movie, "Blue Turtles," and it was very moving. I think that you should go and see it." Then you go home, turn on your TV, and see an advertisement for "Blue Turtles." Later that evening, your mate comes in and says, "I just ran into Bill and Tina. They could not stop talking about the movie, 'Blue Turtles.'" If you are asking God to answer a question, pay attention to things that come up more than three times. That is God's answer. "The question is not, who does God talk to, but rather, who listens?" Neale Donald Walsch, CWG

God loves us unconditionally. We are completely forgiven in the eyes of our creator (no matter what we do, period). However, planet Earth doesn't let you get away with anything. You can try to hide from yourself, but the matrix of God on Earth won't allow it. You might be able to delay it, or put it off for a while, but eventually, the matrix will catch up to you.

Have you ever had an argument with someone or left an issue unresolved? So, what do you do? If you are like me, you just avoid it all together, right?

One day, you decide to go to that specialty shop that is a good 60 miles out of town. This is your favorite place and you know that the person you are in conflict with never goes there. You need to get away from the stress and tension of the situation so you head out to the Winds of Spirit Coffee and Gift House. You feel great; your favorite music is playing on the radio. There is no traffic on the interstate and you just can't wait to get a cup of that incredible joe the restaurant serves. Most important, you know that your friend hates coffee, hates the drive, and is at work. There is no way she is going to be there. As you pull into the driveway of the Winds of Spirit Coffee and Gift House, you think you see your friend's car. You shrug it off as a coincidence. Then you walk into the café and there she is…just to completely ruin your perfect day. No, she is not there to ruin your day; this is the matrix of God at work. This perfect matrix is telling you to stop running and deal with this. I know that all of you have experienced this, because this is the reflective quality of the matrix of God. It reflects back to you where you are in the moment. That is why your life is perfect just the way it is. However, we waste a lot of time and energy focusing on how wrong, messed-up, and screwed up our lives are. Then we want to blame the world, the government, our parents, whomever, instead of seeing our life as a reflection of where we are. The good news is that you can change. As you allow your matrix to change, your life will reflect those changes back to you.

Now, do you see the interconnection of the matrix of God? This is how it works. That is why it is possible to experience miracles. "Ask and so shall you receive." We just don't want to listen. We just don't want to see. We just don't want to believe. Your auric field is constantly bringing to you whatever you project into it. Yet, your matrix is filled with too many imprints, including those from previous lifetimes. Let's say that in a previous lifetime you had one true love. You were "soulmates." The love you shared in that time and place radiated out to everyone around you. Your love was so perfect that it made others jealous, to the point that you were killed—literally stabbed in the back by your own brother—because he wanted your wife for himself. That imprint, that trauma, doesn't die. Energy cannot die; it only transforms, remaining in your matrix or auric field until you clear it. Therefore, you will create relationships based on the belief that people cannot be trusted and you will be betrayed. Again, this is your matrix, the reality that you are tuned into. This is what will be reflected back to you. That is why people are born with birth defects. They are carrying imprints of trauma into their matrix from the time of conception. You may have a genetic predisposition toward a heart defect, but it takes the imprint of a traumatic event to trigger the genetic defect, illness or disease.

I am convinced that our auric field, our matrix field, is so busy reacting to stimuli that it literally prevents the body from healing itself. If your auric field is allergic to medication, then the medication won't work. If your matrix is constantly in fear and terror, your body will break down and all of the traditional treatments will fail. On the other hand, if you change your auric field or matrix field so that it doesn't react to a stimulus but is neutral, your body would automatically heal anything. It is designed to re-create itself. The reactions of our fear-based matrixes prevent it from doing so. For those of you who are skeptical about the ideas and concepts of the auric field, you may want to read *Infinite Mind* by Dr. Valerie Hunt, Ph.D. She is probably the most noted expert on the study of the human auric field.

However, it is vital to understand that all of the imprints in the world cannot compare to the matrix of God—the health, healing, prosperity, abundance, and joy that is within you—right here and right now. We just don't want to see it. No, we want a "big bang," a vision, the big voice. But as a matrix filled with consciousness and aware of all things, the matrix of God takes on all forms and is woven within all things. No amount of karma, astrology, or predestination can compare to the power of a joyous soul that is filled with a pure heart. When you are ONE with the matrix of God, all things become possible.

I can be an immature, irresponsible, manipulative jerk. Yet if the matrix of God flows in my life, then I promise to you that the matrix of God will flow in yours. When you tune into the matrix of God, it goes out of its way to create miracles in your life if you are willing to allow it to do so. You must be willing to ask for it and then let go of how it is going to happen. "How" is none of your business. That is why miracles are called miracles. If you knew how, then miracles would cease to exist. Here are some stories from my life that enable me to say, "I KNOW that the matrix of God is working in my life today."

Since my near death experience, I have had numerous encounters with angels, divas, and entities that most people would call out of the ordinary. A few months ago, I was in Wal-mart to pick up a few things. I saw a young Hispanic couple with their toddler in the aisle next to me. As I approached the young boy, he grinned and said in perfect English, "Deepak Chopra." Needless to say I was in tears. I thought to myself, *how did this young child possibly know anything about Deepak Chopra, let alone know how to pronounce his name correctly?* Here, the young child allowed God to speak through him. It reminded me of who I will become. He was also telling me to stay on the path and don't give up.

A couple of years ago, my life was not working. I was in the "dark night of the soul," as they say. One day I woke up and cried out, "God, I want to hear that I am doing something right for once. I want to hear that I am on the right path. Not only do I want to hear that what I am doing is of value, but I want to hear it from a hot looking Hispanic woman. Not only had she better be hot, she had better be stacked. God! I want 'gazongas' God! Do you understand? Gazongas!"

About an hour later, I was walking to my psychology of communications class and there was a tap on my shoulder. I turned around and a beautiful Hispanic woman looked at me and smiled. "I just wanted to let you know that I really love your radio show and I am glad you are talking about the book Conversations with God. I think that it is great." Yes, God understands what gazongas are.

Also around that time, I was very mad at God. As stated previously, my life was not working. I screamed at God one morning, "I need money! I am broke, God! Money! Cash! NOW! Las Cruces, sucks! God, it fucking sucks! Here I fucking am in Las Clueless, Las fucking Clueless that is. I am stuck, fucking stuck, right in the middle of the goddamn desert!" (Later in this book I will talk about why I was sent to the city of the crosses.) As I continued to rant and rave about the poverty, the act-nothing-do-nothing, manana land of Las Cruces, New Mexico, I received a phone call from a cocaine addict. He felt that hypnosis could help him out with his 10-year addiction.

The following day, he arrived at my office about an hour late. In fact, I was just about to leave as he pulled into the driveway. I thought to my self, *another fucking no-show.* He came with a friend, and was he was jittery. After about 30 minutes, he relaxed. His friend could not believe what he was seeing. "This is amazing," he whispered to me as I took the addict into a deeper, altered state of consciousness. After about an hour, I brought my client out of a very deep trance. He was in tears. He had not experienced that type of relaxation since his addiction began. He hadn't had a line in a week and was on the edge. He finally realized how relaxed he was.

"On my way up here, all that I could think about was doing another line, but that desire is gone. I feel great! Thanks," he said. He proceeded to pull out a wad, and I mean a wad, of one hundred dollar bills. He looked at me and said, "You've helped me, and now I want to help you. Take whatever you want."

I looked at him and said, "What?"

"Take whatever you want, I don't need this any more."

Then I became caught up in my judgements. I thought to myself, *I really need money, but I can't take it because it is drug money.* So, I accepted only what I charge for a session.

Now, stop and think about this. We must confuse the Heaven out of God. Just the other day, I was screaming at God for money. God gives me money and I say no. We ask for what it is that we want, it is given to us, then we reject it. Again, how it happens is none of your business. So, if you are asking for money and you don't want it to be drug money, make sure that you clarify that, got it?

In 1993, I was a waiter at 82 Queen, a charming, romantic fine-dining restaurant in Charleston, South Carolina A man from England came into the restaurant, and for five days in a row ended up in my section. On the last day, I was taking his order and an inner voice said, "Talk to this one about sacred geometry." At the time, I was watching a set of videotapes called, "The Flower of Life," by Drunvalo Melchizedek. These tapes explain the mathematics and origin of life, based on a geometric pattern known as "the flower of life." On that day, we had an hour wait and I was "in the weeds" with six tables. My initial response was, *Yeah, right.* As I walked away, I was pushed back to the front of the table, and again that inner voice said, "Talk to this one about sacred geometry." Reluctantly, I asked him if he was a math teacher.

"Why did you ask me that?" he smiled.

"Well, I am watching these videotapes on sacred geometry right now, which I am sure you have no interest in."

His mouth dropped, "Drunvalo Melchizedek?" As it turned out, he was looking for the same tapes and wanted to know how he could get a set of them. I explained to Rodger that the tapes did not belong to me, but I could put him in touch with the person who gave them to me. We exchanged phone numbers and that night I received a phone call from

Rose Mary—the lady who had lent me the tapes. She said that if it was all right with me, she felt it was important that I give Rodger the set of tapes in my possession. I agreed. The following morning, I met Rodger's son and gave him the tapes.

A few months passed without hearing anything from Rodger or his family. Then, one day, I left work early as it was extremely hot and business was slow. On my way home, that inner voice returned and said, "Please go directly home, we ask that you do not stop anywhere." At the time, Charleston was new to me and I liked to walk around the historic battery and water front. However, I decided to listen and walked directly home. As I opened the door, the phone rang. It was Rodger, calling me from France. He explained that Drunvalo was going to be in Cope Crest, North Carolina, and wanted to know if I would like to go. Without hesitation, I said, "YES!" I wanted to know how much it was going to cost and if I could get tickets.

"Don't worry," he said, " it has all been taken care of. Everything has been paid for. Thank you for the set of tapes. Enjoy."

So, from November 13th through 19th, 1993, I attended an incredible workshop given by Drunvalo Melchizedek. Why? Because I was willing to allow the matrix of God do the work. I just listened, trusted, and took action. There are no accidents or coincidences. "God doesn't roll dice with the Universe." (Albert Einstein) The universe can and will orchestrate miracles for you if you simply get out of the way. In my opinion, the flower of life and the mer-ka-ba are the matrixes of God within all things. They are "The Force."

In 1995, I needed a place to stay. I still worked at 82 Queen. As I walked into the magnificent courtyard I thought, *God I need a place to stay. I cannot pay a deposit, nor can I sign a lease. I must be compatible with the roommate and I can only pay $350 or less a month.* As I finished that thought, the owner, Joe S., looked at me and said, "I just sat you four tables, get ready." From the moment that I walked into the door until I left, I was busy. I made more than $200 that night. I was so busy that I completely forgot about what I had asked for earlier that evening. When I went home, there was a message on my answering machine. "Mark this is Darianne. I need a roommate—you don't have to pay a deposit, you don't have to sign a lease, there is no long term commitment. It is $325 a month. Can you move in this weekend?"

In 1996, I went to register for fall classes at New Mexico State University. The lady at the registrar's office informed me that I could not enroll for fall classes since I still owed monies from the previous semester. Now, at no time did she see the list of classes I wanted to take. Even if she did, she couldn't have recorded them since the system automatically places a block on registration documents when accounts are not up to date. I went to the financial aid office, picked up my student loan money, proceeded to the accounts receivable office, and paid my tuition bill. After lunch, I returned to the registrar's office to complete my registration. On my way there, I called out in my inner mind, *God if you really want me to complete my degree, give me a sign, because quite frankly God, school sucks the big one.*

With my registration documents in hand, the lady at the terminal asked me for my student I.D. number. As she entered the number into the computer, something amazing happened. Low and behold, I was registered for all of the classes that were on my registration paper—the ones she had never seen nor entered into the computer. They were listed in the same order as on my paper, at the same times, and with the teachers that I had selected, without a single "class closed" marker. Her mouth dropped and she shook her head in disbelief as she said, "Someone up there is watching over you."

I responded, "Yes, that is becoming more and more apparent to me."

You see, my registration had been done through me. It was already done. When Jesus raised Lazarus and walked on water, he never said or thought, "Oh shit, how is this going to happen?" Rather, he KNEW that it was already done through him. Jesus's faith in the matrix of God that is within was so great that it became a KNOWING. Jesus demonstrated his KNOWING. "Be still and KNOW that I Am." Be still and KNOW that I AM WITHIN YOU. The only thing that we are here to do is to demonstrate our KNOWING.

Unfortunately, we have learned to demonstrate our matrixes of fears, doubts, and disbeliefs. We have forgotten to remember our connection to the matrix of God that is within us. True salvation is about remembering our connection to our souls. As we connect with our inner being, we begin to connect with the matrix of God. As we connect with our soul, we begin to see all life as a reflection of us. Life is our mirror, showing us where we have not yet learned to demonstrate our knowing. Every person you meet will reflect back to you the areas you have not yet mastered. Therefore, all life becomes a matrix, showing you all aspects of yourself, especially those parts that you would rather not look at. Which matrix do you want to tune into? Which matrix are you willing to allow yourself to see?

Chapter Three

Messages From the Masters

Yes, I have had many visitors in the dream state who speak to me. Jesus, Mother Mary, Thoth, Isis, but most frequently it is John the Baptist. I first heard of John the Baptist from a close friend of mine, Patty Lou Fetters. She played me a recording of the "Out of the Ordinary Show" from KIEV in Los Angeles, California. According to the host, Joe Albiani, Gerry Bowman entered into a trance state and channeled an entity who called himself John the Baptist. Shortly after listening to a few shows, John found his way into my dreams and began relaying many messages, both for myself and humanity. Even though some of these will read as if John is talking to me directly, he is actually speaking to everyone, including you.

Messages from John the Baptist

- A master is not called a master because he himself says so. A master is called a master because those who witness him say that he is master.
- We never use the truth to be right, we never use the truth to score points for our
  Ego, and we never use the truth to make others wrong.
- The Kingdom of God is within you. Why do you seek anything else?

- If one would live in the moment, what fear would they have? What fear could they have?

- Why do you worry? It does not matter what name you may give it or how you may call it. Rejoice, for the lord is always with you. Rejoice, for the lord made this day. Just realize the lord that we are talking about here is YOU.
- Love is who you are. Be Love.
- Why do you seek that which you already are? (Why seek God? Rather, become God.)
- Power cannot be given unto a child. However, you must become like a child before you can receive the power that you seek.

This refers to the difference between "childish" and "child-like." "Except ye be converted and become as little children, ye shall not enter the Kingdom of God." Children are fully present in the moment, are playful and spontaneous, and always tell the truth. Most importantly, they use their imagination.

> To see life through the eyes of a child
> Everything is new, everything has meaning
> Questions are asked, answers are yet to behold
> Colors are brighter
> Sight has insight
> And tasting becomes a cosmos
> Colors, Smells, Tastes, Experiences
> and this Overflow
> Is not enough to quench the thirst of Curiosity
> Sensations Perceptions and Emotions
> Without Knowledge
> There is only an Innate Trust
> That the World is a Safe Place
> Life from these Eyes is true Living

—Mark Patterson

- If you want to see God, then look in the mirror.
- If others label you as inadequate, that is their problem, not yours.
- Expansion is that what you fear. Allow your creativity to flow, dear child, allow your creativity to flow.
- See the light in the mirror. As you learn to love that light in the reflection of the mirror, you will come to know that you are a wonderful human being with much to share.
- When you are willing to accept yourself, as you are now, in the moment, you will become very powerful.
- Do you really want to experience your life as anything less than Jesus?
- You view surrendering as a weakness. Surrendering is a great strength. For both our strengths and our weaknesses become diluted into one with Love.
- You are the beloved and we rejoice in your presence.
- Love yourself
- There is not a single moment that goes by in your life that you are alone. You are never alone dear child, never. We are always with you.
- Learn to see yourself in all things, all people, and all places. Your life is a direct reflection of you. Here is an example:

Two different people look at the same picture. They both see the same shapes, colors, and textures. One person says the picture is incredible and delights in it. The other person hates it, complaining that it is too simple. These are two different responses to the same picture. But are they really seeing the same picture? Or are they seeing themselves as reflected through that picture, that person, that place, that object? Life then becomes your mirror. It will reflect back to you all aspects of yourself. Learn to see what is being reflected back to you. Use life to show you to yourself, for we are all ONE.

- If you were wise enough to know, what question would you ask? (The answer, of course, is contained within the question. If you were wise enough to KNOW, you wouldn't ask the question in the first place.)
- You already know the answers to the questions that you ask. Validation? Is that what you seek? Validation? Trust, dear child, trust and know that who you are and what you do is important and of tremendous value.
- Service to mankind is always first.
- Stop being a martyr to your own joy. It is simply not necessary unless you choose it. If you choose it, then so be it, but it is not necessary.
- There is nothing that you cannot change. You may not know how or why you created it, but once you accept that you chose it, then you can change it. There is NOTHING that you cannot change (unless you become victimized by it). Be not the victim, be the creator.
- Why do you allow others to determine your worthiness? You are worthy simply because you are.
- Allow your feelings of inadequacy to be what they are, for they can move you and guide you into a place of power.
- Why do you bring the past into the present? Now is all there is. Does the past really matter right here, right now? NO, then DROP it!

- We want you to look in the mirror and say "I LOVE YOU."
- Why do you fear love?
- Why do you measure and compare yourself to others? Do you think that God does?
- If one is in their head with another, then you are really not with the other individual.
- The plan is there is NO PLAN. There is ONLY NOW.

- The end of the world is at hand, but which world are we speaking of? Physical mental, or emotional? (I believe that the mental world—duality consciousness—is about to come to an end)
- Life is a gift. You are a gift to the world. Your gift to the world is your gift to God.
- Guilt and shame are like a ruse, a facade that hides the light from you. What is there that you cannot love within yourself?
- When you see the light in other people, you will see the light in yourself.
- "When you see the Son in the Father, you will see the Father in the Son."
- You may think that you can start completely over by moving to a new location. Just realize that you take yourself wherever you go. (Wherever you go, there you are.)

- Enlightenment looks just like this. It looks just like this room, or this wall. Enlightenment is not something that you over-achieve into. It is something that you allow. Relax into it. Do you think that you are going to create "super flatulence?"
- Throw away the cape. (Stop trying to save everyone. Save yourself first.)
- Meditation is how you focus your attention. As you learn to focus your energy towards one goal, your life will become very productive. You tend to divert your energy into too many different things. This is not a race. There is nowhere to go. You will always be here.
- You have learned to listen to your inner voice, now listen to your heart.

Messages from Jesus

- Tell them to take me off the cross. I can no longer carry their pain. It was never my job to do so in the first place. (The crucifixion is a metaphor that was used by many cultures prior to Christianity. It symbolizes the burdens one carries for others. What are you placing on your heart that does not belong? Jesus carried the burden of showing that death was an illusion, as he did not die on the cross but resurrected.)

- Why do you not believe in the miracle of the NOW? Why do you not believe in the miracle that is you? Why do you not open your heart to the divine that is within? Within your heart is where you will find me.

As a child, I used to dream that I was inside my bedroom closet, which contained all the gifts and toys I could ever possibly want. Anytime that I felt lonely, unwanted or rejected, I found myself inside that magical closet. Anything that I wanted was there waiting for me. It has taken me 25 years to realize the story behind that dream. Everything that I, or you, could ever want is contained within the closet of your own heart. "Above all things first ye seek the Kingdom of God." Yes, that magical place is within all of us, right here, right now.

- You are LOVED.
- When you listen to your heart, you will find God.
- Be still.
- Yes, it is true that I said, "I am the way and I am the truth." But that did not mean that you could not do it without me. For you are also the light, the way, and the truth. I just left a pattern that was to be followed.

Do you understand this? Please allow me to rephrase it. You can get to God just as you are, right now. You don't have to believe that Jesus is your savior, nor do you need to believe in Buddha, Krishna, Sai Baba, or any Baba. However, if you can't believe that you can do it by yourself, then you can do it through Jesus. Unfortunately, the church forgot to mention that you could do it by yourself. They focused on the part that said that you had to do it through him. (Actually, it seems that the church forgot to mention a lot of what Jesus taught) John 10:34: "Is it not written in your laws, I say ye are Gods." Again, the church became caught up in the messenger, not his message.)

- There are only opportunities to learn forgiveness.
- Why do you not believe? Faith in your self is the key!
- I am with you.
- There is only love and fear. Fear is the absence of love.
- I am not the answer, love is.

Messages from my Angels
- Here are messages from my angels. For the most part they are talking to me. However, many of these messages will apply to you.
- Listen to the music of your own being.
- Trust the inner voices of your own being.
- It gives us great pleasure to hear your thanks, as your thanks is music to our ears.
- Going within on a daily basis will be of great benefit.
- Foods that are of nature are more fueling for the body.
- Meat and dairy products will cloud your visionary body.
- How we long to hold you; how we long for you to KNOW that we are holding you.
- You take yourself way too seriously.
- Play more.
- Sex is important to us and there are quiet a few of us feminine angels who would love to have sex with you. So, stop pretending that women find you unattractive. As long as you believe that women find you unattractive, you can be safe and not experience love. Surround yourself with women. There is nothing guilty or shameful about sex. We envy your ability to achieve orgasm. Sex is a great gift. However, we caution you that it is not to be misused. (I was 20 and very shy when they told me this.)
- We are you.

34 • You Are God

- You cannot comprehend how beautiful you are from our perspective. We do not see your body, we see your soul. That is indeed a sight to behold.
- There are many beings about you. The divas and fairies play around your hands. They will always bring you good luck.
- You came here with many memories of the future. It's as if you know what is about to happen just before it does.
- Acting "overly special" is the misuse of energy and it will return itself upon you.
- You are not alone.
- Act as if you are in awe of life. Make every moment sacred.
- Stop punishing yourself.
- Trust your inner guidance; you have a tendency to dismiss it.
- You are like a child who wants to play at the amusement park all day, but one of these days you will need to grow up.

Messages from Mother Mary
- We want you to know that you are loved UNCONDITIONALLY.
- Dear child, know that you are loved.
- You are blessed. You have many gifts. Use them, for they are needed.
- Trust that you have it within to create whatever it is you are wanting.
- Trust the process of life. Even when it appears that you cannot, trust.
- We are joyous in your presence.
- You cannot fathom the love that we have for you.
- You are protected. You are safe. You are wanted.

A message from Thoth

Thoth was an Egyptian God. According to Drunvalo Melchizedek, Thoth provided all of the information that is taught in the Flower of Life workshops.

- You humans forget how important you are to us. You send us information, just as we send you information. We (the ascended masters) could not complete our work without you.

A message from Kryon

Kryon is an entity channeled by Lee Carroll. Kryon came to me in a dream one night after I listened to one of Lee's tapes. I perceived Kryon as electromagnetic waves shaped like a tube torus (i.e., a doughnut). Kryon literally blasted a wave of energy into my etheric body, which contained a very simple message:

- Feel the love that your inner being has for you. Always focus on it and you will do great things. Kryon then left.

I woke up glowing, feeling wonderful. I think that most people have found that their lives have been more chaotic during the past few years. Americans seem to be losing it emotionally. Have you noticed that time has shifted into warp speed, that there doesn't seem to be enough hours in the day to get everything done? I look into people's faces and see exhaustion and burnout. While Wall Street continues to expand and thrive, nearly 40 million people live in poverty in the U.S. I am going to paraphrase something Kryon said in a recent article that finally made sense. I have seen this in many people.

> Before most of you came here, your inner being knew that between 1996-1999 this time frame would be the "end of times," as you would call it. Within, you created an imprint of self-termination that was to be activated during these times. Yet all of you have now shifted this need to self terminate, but the imprint is still there. Because you have shifted this need to self-terminate, you have also activated within you a new strand of DNA. Now you are dealing with a new DNA that is instructing you to go forward while the imprint of self-termination is fading away. You literally have within your body an energy that it was never designed to carry.

36 • You Are God

This explains a lot. If you think that this idea of self-termination is crazy, here is another quote from Tara Sutphen who is channeling her spirit guide, Abend:

> There is a will within many to destroy what they have, because with survival comes a sense of belonging to the earth and all that it means. Rather than focusing upon survival, it is time to live in your world. Open your mind, your eyes and your senses to what all life can be. It is your divine right. Accept your right and you will know the path of life.

Again, that is why we must address the "dark" that is within us. In truth, love is the answer. As you learn to love all aspects of yourself, you will integrate your own darkness. The plan of light within you will prevail.

A message from Abraham

Abraham is channeled by Ester and Jerry Hicks. I was walking to class one day when Abraham came to me and said: "Do you really think that you are more intelligent than God? Trust life Mark, trust the process. All is well in your life and you are guided. Trust."

Indeed, I am guided and these are just a few of the messages that I have received from our nonphysical friends. I wish I could trust their guidance more, and ultimately trust my own heart and soul. There seems to be a fine line between our guides guiding us, and our guides steering us off the path as a test, to see if we will listen to them or trust ourselves. I am reminded of a conversation that I had with my friend, Sherry, the other day. We happened to receive the same information on this very subject.

Your guides will change their advice as your awareness changes. Here is an example. For the past year, I have been focusing on going to Naropa University for my master of arts degree in Transpersonal Psychology. Transpersonal psychology excites me; I am passionate about it. Transpersonal psychology looks at a person from a holistic perspective— body, mind and soul. It gets to the cause of a problem rather than just treating the symptoms. My guides have been pushing me to go to Naropa. Unfortunately, a degree in transpersonal psychology is not taken seriously in our society; I would probably be laughed at. Then, my awareness shifted. I thought, Why not get a masters degree in Industrial and Organizational Psychology? I could apply transpersonal and spiritual concepts in corporate settings where they are the most needed. The people who are into transpersonal psychology are going to see me. The people who are not will avoid me like the plague. With this degree, I could reach more people and become a trainer in group dynamics.

Wouldn't it be great to have a spiritual environment at companies such as Microsoft, Dell, Intel, IBM, GM, and Ford? Wouldn't be wonderful if the corporate world placed a sanctuary in every building? Wouldn't it be great if corporate decisions were made through a relationship with a "higher power"? Now, this gets me excited. I have a stronger sense of purpose now. I have something to focus on. This also gets my angels excited; they guide me as I follow this plan. I will continue to study transpersonal psychology on the side and incorporate it into my work. As you shift your awareness, your guidance follows that shift. And so it is.

Chapter four

Religion's Dark Side

The TV evangelists, the fundamentalists, born-agains, the Catholic Church, and most Christians have the masses convinced that there is only one way to discover God—their God, that is. They want you to believe that Jesus died on the cross for your sins and that you will die and burn in Hell unless you claim him as your personal savior. They want you to think that you can do whatever you want to in this life and just before you die, proclaim that you have accepted Jesus into your life. By doing this, you will be saved and can go to Heaven and avoid burning in Hell. There are some crucial errors in this thinking.

1) Jesus did NOT die on the cross. He RESURRECTED.

2) The Bible is NOT God's word. It is the word of inspired WHITE men, subject to endless interpretation. Most of the original ARAMAIC bible has been long forgotten and never revealed.

3) Man is NOT a sinner, nor is he born in sin. John 10:34: "Is it not written in your laws, I say, yea are GODS." We are GODS, and the Catholic Church has suppressed this truth to control the masses through FEAR/GUILT/SHAME.

4) The Second Coming CANNOT HAPPEN because HE NEVER LEFT!

5) The Kingdom of Heaven is within us, it is us, and therefore WE DO NOT NEED TO DIE IN ORDER TO EXPERIENCE IT!

6) What Jesus taught and what the Christian/Catholic Church says he taught are two different things.

Now, let's look at some historical facts!

First, Jesus, or Joshua, was an ESSENE. Mary and Joseph were ESSENES. Because of this, Jesus would have taught about karma and reincarnation.

Second, the Gnostic Christians—the first followers of Jesus—also taught about karma and reincarnation.

Third, the original symbol for Jesus was NOT the crucifixion, but rather, a dolphin. (I will explain why this is important later in this chapter.)

Fourth, 2,000 years ago in the Middle East, the term for a young woman was "VIRGO." This was changed or translated to mean "VIRGIN." Mary was a VIRGO, NOT A VIRGIN.

Also, there were NO Caucasians in the Middle East 2,000 years ago. Thus, Jesus would have had a dark or olive complexion. So, this whole idea that the white race is superior because God's only son was white is a bunch of buffalo chips.

The people who knew Jesus knew nothing about humans living in other areas of the planet. Even though there were people in Africa, North and South America and elsewhere, they did not exist in the minds of those who witnessed the times and life of Jesus, including the crucifixion. Therefore, when it is said, "He died on the cross for man's sins," it could have only applied to contemporaries of Jesus.

You must realize that most of us have been taught HISTORY (His-story) from a white, European perspective. To this day, we still teach our children that Christopher Columbus discovered America. Yet this is a blatant lie. Can you imagine what it would be like if history was taught from a Native American perspective? We might be taught that Christopher Columbus invaded or ruined America. Indeed, we are so egocentric.

Fifth, karma and reincarnation were removed from the teachings of Christianity and the Catholic Church in 553 A.D. at the Second Council of Constantinople by the Nicene decree. This conflict arose between Roman Emperor Justine and Origen's doctrine of reincarnation. "Anyone who believes in the pre-existing soul shall be left in anathema or exiled from the church." The Catholic Church declared Origen's doctrine of reincarnation to be heresy, as well as the Thirteenth Gospel, written by Jesus. However, more than 80 percent of all religions teach about karma and reincarnation.

Finally, the Bible was not translated into English until 1738 A.D. All of you know what happens when you tell a story to someone, and that story gets passed onto the next person, and the next…by the time it reaches the 10th person, the original story is distorted at best. Now, if 10 people can't get the original story straight, what do you think would happen to a story that was passed down for more than 1,700 years?

Historically speaking, the Catholic Church has committed the most heinous atrocities against the human race. "The Pope doesn't kill." EXCUSE ME. The Catholic Church nearly eliminated an entire race of beings—the Native Americans—on not ONE, but TWO, continents. This was also true in the "dark ages," when the church destroyed the Egyptian mystery schools and the teachings of the Egyptian God, Hathor. Later on, it killed off the Pagans and Celtics, and continued its persecution with the Salem witch-hunts. We have been taught that St. Patrick's Day is about St. Patrick, who killed all the snakes in Ireland. There are no snakes in Ireland, only Pagans who were labeled as snakes. This behavior continued into WW II, with Hitler labeling the Jews as "snakes." He killed six million human beings because of this type of thinking.

Who made the Catholic Church judge and jury of this planet we call Earth? Who? And by what law? What right do you have to decide that others are evil and then kill them? And you kill in the name of GOD? "My God is right and yours is wrong. Think as we do or die in Hell. We are saved and chosen; you are not." These are people who claim to be saved? People who claim to be chosen—how arrogant are you, really? The people of the Jewish faith say that they are the chosen ones.

Christian/Catholics say that no, they are the saved ones. The Islamic fundamentalist say that The Koran is the book of God and that Allah is God.

Considering that all of these people are saved and chosen, we sure have a lot of conflicts in the world today. Look at the Catholics and Protestants. Look at the Middle East. Look at what just happened in the former Yugoslavia. It is this type of thinking that causes all wars and conflicts in the world. I ask, how can it possibly be right? Religions keep people divided,. not united. We are all ONE. "Even when you hurt the least of your brethren, you hurt me." WE ARE ALL ONE. I had a NEAR DEATH EXPERIENCE 14 years ago. In Heaven there is NO religion, there is ONLY GOD.

The greatest crime ever committed against the human race was to tell man that he was a sinner and unworthy to receive God's love. The amount of irreversible damage, separation, hatred, and division that this has caused cannot possibly be measured.

To teach people that we are sinners born in sin, to deny that we are Gods, and to suppress the truth that the Kingdom of Heaven is within us right here and right now, is BLASPHEMOUS. "Judge NOT that ye be judged, for the judgment that you have is the judgment you shall receive, and the measure you give shall be the measure you shall get. GOD IS LOVE. LOVE CANNOT JUDGE, PERIOD. As the above quote states, we are not judged. However, we sow and we reap. This is KARMA. "Judge NO ONE, for you do not know how they stand in the eyes of GOD." In telling someone that they need to be saved—is this not a judgment? What are you doing?

Jesus was a master of his own thoughts. His faith in himself was so great and he was so tuned into the matrix of GOD, that when he raised Lazarus he never said, "How am I going to do this?" Rather he KNEW that it was already done through him. He demonstrated his KNOWING. All of the tests in life occur in areas where you have not yet learned to demonstrate your KNOWING, lifetime after lifetime after lifetime. Jesus was a savior, not because he died on the cross, but because he showed us how to end the cycle of karma and reincarnation. This is done through compassion, forgiveness, non-judgement, and unconditional love. (Yes, I am repeating myself here, but it is so important that you get this.)

Yet the Christian/Catholic Church is all about JUDGMENT, JUDGMENT AND MORE JUDGMENT. It is caught up in the messenger, not his message. "Love God and love your brother." If we are Gods like HE said, then the real truth is, "LOVE YOURSELF SO THAT YOU MAY IN TURN LOVE YOUR BROTHER."

"God loved us so much that he sent his only Son…" What does this have to do with love? Would you send your only child to a distant planet, knowing that he would be killed by the time he was 33? This has nothing to do with love, NOTHING! It is the biggest guilt trip ever placed on the consciousness of the human race. So, if you are trying to save someone out of love, STOP. It is NOT LOVE. It is a judgment based in fear and control, and it feeds on people's feelings of guilt and shame.

Rather, teach people that we are all ONE, that the Kingdom of Heaven is within us right here, right now, and that we are God's. This, and only this, will end all wars, hatred, separation, and conflict. GET OUT OF RELIGION AND GET INTO GOD. That GOD is YOU. True salvation is about remembering your connection to your own soul, the Kingdom of Heaven that is within you right here, right now. Follow your soul, listen to your heart, and to thine own self be true. This is about following the matrix of the inner Christ, the matrix that Jesus left for us. Since we are all ONE, if one can do it, all can do it.

Jesus left a matrix for us to follow, a pattern that would enable us to become like him. "Even greater miracles then these, ye shall do as well." This is why many "new thought" or "new age" churches (i.e., Science of Mind or Unity) refer to Jesus as the "Way Shower" rather than a savior. In my opinion, this is far more accurate.

This is just a side note that I think you will find interesting: The Dogons are a remote tribe of people from the west coast of Africa who have an oral history that goes back 50,000 years. During the past five years, numerous physicists and astronomers have visited the Dogons because of their accurate information on various star systems..Although by our standards they should not know about such things, they specifically know about two star systems Sirius A and Sirius B.

Everything that the Dogons have said has been scientifically confirmed. They obviously did a better job of storytelling than the Catholic Church, because the story was kept within the tribe and did not cross language and cultural barriers. So, what does this have to do with Jesus? According to the Dogons, Jesus came from the Planet Sirius and was a dolphin. This explains why the original symbol for Jesus was a dolphin. The story of the fish and loaves of bread did not come about until 400 years after his death.

Why is it that we know nothing of Jesus' life after the resurrection? Wouldn't that be the most IMPORTANT? But that, too, was suppressed, because it is the only way that the Christian/Catholic Church could say that he "died on the Cross..." Now, back to this Jesus as a dolphin concept. I believe that if Jesus came to you and you were ill, you would be cured instantly. Does anyone know what happens when people who are ill with multiple sclerosis, cancer, or most other illnesses swim with dolphins? They are instantly cured. Kinda makes you wonder, doesn't it?

(Today is March 12, 2000, and it is interesting to see that the Pope is asking for forgiveness for the church's sins. How ironic.)

Chapter Five

Knowing the Matrix of God

Wherever you are in your life, regardless of what is happening, stop and say, "Thank You God." Say it again, "Thank You God." Now, say it with a heart that is filled with joy and proclaims, "Thank You God."

A few months ago, I had a very interesting dream that demonstrates the power of gratitude. In the dream, I was at a workshop where a woman was giving a lecture on angels and how to connect with the I Am Presence. She had this "I am above it all" attitude, since she was able to communicate with angels. The woman continued to profess how spiritual she was. She spoke of her pure organic diet and shared that she didn't drink coffee, smoke or drink alcohol. She made everyone in that room know that she was a Goddess of light. She proclaimed that she was a "Divine Minister of the Angelic Light" and that drinking coffee, smoking or drinking alcohol were only done by "lower" people. (I call these people "new age dough-nuts." They are light and fluffy on the outside, but completely empty on the inside.)

In the dream, I approached the speaker with a cup of coffee in my hand and began to move objects with my mind. I then put my hand gently through a wall and pulled it back out, and waved my right hand in the air to demonstrate that there were numerous angels around me. She looked at me in complete dismay and disgust and asked, "How is it possible that a lower person like you can create miracles and me, this great master, cannot?" (Now, this is what I want you to get, so pay attention.)

In the dream I looked at her and said, "My coffee drinking, wine drinking, playboy persona and professional-wrestling-watching ass will always create miracles. Not even on your best day will you ever have the passion, enthusiasm, excitement, and sincere appreciation for life that I do." Whoooooo! I woke up and thought to myself, *wow, that really says it all, having sincere appreciation for life itself.*

As a psychology major, I have been exposed to Abraham Maslow's hierarchy of needs in just about every psychology class I have taken. It is a theory that says that if lower physiological needs are met—food, water, and shelter—then belonging needs can be met. If a person feels that he is loved, then he can feel good about himself. If a person's self esteem needs are met, then she can develop a sense of purpose. If she fulfills this purpose then she can achieve self-actualization, which is the ability to fully live to one's highest potential.

After years of studying these concepts, I have wondered why more people don't achieve self-actualization. I then came across some more information on Abraham Maslow. According to Maslow, one of the key elements of self-actualization is a sincere appreciation for life in and of itself. Now, why is it that we are rarely taught this when studying Maslow? After all, we have been exposed to Maslow's hierarchy of needs since middle school. I believe that this is one of the main reasons that very few people achieve self-actualization. When studying Maslow, we are not taught his concept regarding the importance of a sincere appreciation for life itself.

It must have been in November 1998, when something happened which I will never forget. I was making a pot of herbal tea and looking at the boiling water in complete awe. In that state, I began to say in my inner mind, *Thank you, thank you, thank you, thank you, thank you, thank you.* Then I looked at the ceiling and it continued. *Thank you, thank you, thank you, thank you, thank you, thank you.* Then I was on my knees in tears, looking at my kitchen and shouting, "Thank you, thank you, thank you, thank you, thank you, thank you." My friends, nothing will shift your focus from "I am a victim" to self-actualization to the matrix of God faster than saying thank you. Now I give thanks for everything. My inner being doesn't stop. It won't let me stop. *Thank you, thank you, thank you, thank you, thank you, thank you.* (It is doing it right now, as I am writing this.)

The second thing that will lead you to self-actualization and the matrix of God is passion. "Passion is the key to self-actualization," according to Neale Donald Walsch, CWG. (Conversations with God) I am not talking about sexual passion, but about passion and enthusiasm for life itself. I am talking of being passionate and excited about who you are and what you do.

I have a 40-pound female pit-bull named Cherokee. She was the runt of the litter, but snapped a 2,600 pound test cable just a month ago. Cherokee is full of passion, excitement, and enthusiasm. I admire and envy her attitude towards life. I recall a day when she accidentally destroyed a glass clock that was sitting on a bookcase because she was so excited to see me. I was about to hit her but stopped myself. This is exactly what happens to us when we demonstrate our passion for life as children. It usually gets beaten out of us and we learn to suppress the truth of what we want to do. We end up placing our second foot forward, so to speak.

I am convinced that we are born to win and conditioned to lose. We are born winners, not sinners. We are children of God, placed here to be dynamic, creative, and passionate, but conditioned to feel unworthy, guilty, and unwanted.

There is a story in the Book of Peter in the Bible, in which Peter is on the ocean or a body of water. Soon the water becomes unstable and a storm develop. The waves become treacherous and Peter calls out to God. Immediately, Jesus appears to him, 10 to 15 feet away, and standing on the water. Jesus calls out to Peter, "Come to me." Peter focuses his attention on Jesus and begins to walk on the water towards him, despite the storm. Unfortunately, Peter soon returns his focus to the storm. In doing so, he begins to sink and again calls out, "Help me God." Jesus pulls Peter out of the water and saves him.

Do you understand the metaphor of this story? The ocean or body of water represents our emotional body—our matrix of fear, troubles, worries, and problems that life reflects back to us. When we focus on the matrix of God that is within us as Jesus, we can rise above our emotional problems. But as soon as we re-focus on the matrix of fear, we become overwhelmed by it. Always, always, always, focus on the matrix of God that is within. I would like to share with you some powerful "I am statements" that can only lead to miracles in your life.

- I am thankful for miracles in my life!
- I am thankful for financial miracles in my life!
- I am thankful for being healed!
- I am thankful for God in my life!
- I am thankful for being successful!
- I am thankful for being wanted!
- I am thankful for being in harmony with the universe!
- I am thankful for thought and ideas that lead me to the path that I intended before I came here!
- I am thankful for being an inspiration to others!
- I am thankful for being supported!

- I am thankful for being in my ideal relationship!
- I am thankful for being recognized by my peers!
- I am thankful for my life!
- I am thankful for being one with the matrix of God!
- I am thankful for demonstrating my knowing!
- I am thankful for inner peace, balance, and harmony!
- I am thankful that my services are in demand!
- I am thankful!

It is also important you ask for help with this process. Ask and you shall receive. Thus, it pays to know how to ask for the right things. Several years ago, I said, "You know God, I want a beautiful woman to come up to me from behind and reach around and grab my crotch and say, 'Let's find out what you got in here, stranger.'" In a dream later that evening, I received my wish. I woke up laughing because I received exactly what I'd asked for, but I didn't clarify that I wanted it in the physical. I think God is a real jokester at times.

Some suggestions about what to ask for are listed below. First, imagine that you have an entire army of angels longing to hear your command. Second, imagine that they will go out of their way to help you obtain whatever it is you want. Third, have faith and trust that it will be given to you. If you use this technique to manipulate someone or to get them to fall in love with you, chances are it is not going to work. Never use this to try to destroy or kill someone. The best time to do this is in the morning when you first wake up.

- Show me that I am a success in the physical.
- Show me that I am wanted in the physical.
- Show me that I am capable in the physical.
- Show me that I am loved in the physical.
- Show me what I am to do with my life in the physical.
- Give me thoughts and ideas which lead me on the path that I intended to follow before I came here.
- Connect me with people of like mind in the physical.
- Give me words and ideas to inspire others today.
- Show me things that help me feel good about myself in the physical.
- Show me my creativity in the physical.
- Show me where I am to go next in the physical.

I am sure that you can come up with your own "I am thankful" and "show me" statements. All things are possible within the matrix of God.

It is important that you ask to receive things in safe and loving ways. Here is a story which illustrates this point. There was once a young man who was very angry at God. His life was no longer fulfilling and he demanded that God create a miracle in his life. He kept yelling at God: "I want $50,000!" "I need $50,000!" The ranting and raving continued for a month or so. Soon after the emotional rampage ended, the young man lost his leg in a bad car accident. Six weeks after the accident, he received a check from his insurance company for $50,000! So, be very clear about what you want, ask for it in safe and loving ways, have faith you will receive it, and know that you are worthy to receive it.

This brings us to one of the most important topics in this book—self-worth. There is nothing more important than feeling good about yourself. How many of you know people who attend one self-help, motivational workshop after the next? Yet no matter how much money that they spend, their life still sucks. How many of you know people who have studied *A Course in Miracles* for 20 or 30 years and their life still remains status-quo? How many of you know individuals who give until they literally have nothing and receive very little in return? Yet, Jesus said, "As you give, so shall you receive."

Why is it that these principles and workshops seem to work for some but fail for a vast majority of others? The answer to this question is simple. If you are not getting what you want out of life, you need to look at you feelings of self-worth. If at a core level you feel unworthy to receive, all of the self-help books, motivational talks, and inspirational studies combined will not help you change your life. This is why I stated in an earlier chapter that the greatest crime ever committed against the human race was to label man a sinner, guilty and unworthy to receive God's love. In my opinion, deep-seated feelings of unworthiness and loneliness are at the core of all addictions and problems in society. If you feel unworthy and guilty, you are literally rejecting your ability to receive the life you want. You are rejecting the truth that "it is God's good pleasure to grant you the Kingdom." You are literally rejecting yourself.

You must be willing to give whatever it is you want first to yourself, before you can receive it from others. Thus, if you want recognition, you must recognize the child of God that is you. If you want approval, you must be pleased with yourself. If you want others to listen to you, you must be willing to listen to the voice of your own heart. If you want to be accepted, you must be willing to accept yourself as you are in the moment.

It is your state of "beingness" that creates your reality. If you feel guilty, then you are being guilty. If you feel resentful, then you are being resentful. If you feel hatred, then you are being hateful. If you feel unworthy, you are being unworthy. If you are being unworthy, how can you possibly receive what you are asking for? Thus, the matrix of your beingness creates the experience. Again, this matrix will attract and reflect back to you your state of beingness. If you have financial problems, it is merely a reflection of your feelings of insecurity. If you feel insecure, you are being insecure. Thus, if you want to transform your life, you must free yourself from the bonds and shackles of loneliness, guilt, and unworthiness. This is what Jesus meant when he said, "I have come here to set the captives free."

You remain bound in your own prison of guilt and shame. However, if you are willing to open up and recognize the "Inner Christ," then the matrix of God will set the captives free. It took me a long time to realize that as long as I held my father in my own mental prison for being a failure, for not being there for me, and for living at home his entire life, I sat in the jail cell with him. You will suffer along with whoever you hold in captivity, because whatever you resist will persist. There is a Zen story that goes like this:

> Two young Zen students are resting under a Gobi tree. One looks at the other and says, "I have fasted, and meditated for weeks. I have given up food. I still suffer. I have given up all of my worldly possessions to God. I still suffer. I have given up sex, drugs, rock and roll. I still suffer. I have given up my life to God and to this stupid

philosophy. I still suffer." Before he could say another word, the other student looked at him and said, "Give up suffering."

Second, you may be asked to give what you want in life to another before you are allowed to receive it. If you want a mate who is financially secure, you may be asked to provide financial security to another. You can only get out of life what you put into it.

This brings us to a point that is often missed in self-help workshops. If you really want to change your life and your state of beingness, you must be willing to change your actions. If you are digging yourself into a hole, one of the first things that you must do is to stop digging. Most self-help workshops focus on changing your thinking and attitude, but in order to eliminate the self-sabotage in your life, you must take a different action. Once you take a different action, you set into place and anchor a new matrix that enables you to create the life you want.

If you have issues of unworthiness, one of the first things you can do is change your behavior at a restaurant. If you receive something you don't want, or if it is not to your liking, send it back. This action says to the Universe: "I am worthy to receive what I have asked for." Once you change your action, you are proclaiming to God that you are serious about transforming the quality of your life. I am sure that many of you have heard the analogy that the Universe works like a restaurant. When you place an order, you don't think about how is it going to arrive at your table. You don't worry about whether it will be the way that you want. No, you sit back and relax; you allow it too happen. Your state of beingness is hunger. You ask for—and receive—what you want, pay your bill and go on your way, satisfied.

Isn't your state of beingness in life similar? Aren't all of you longing at a core level to remember who you are? Aren't you hungry for something more? Unfortunately, we get in our own way because we want to know how we are going to get what we want. Again, "how" is none of your business. When you combine this with feelings of unworthiness, life can

52 • You Are God

sometimes appear hopeless. Realize that, just as in a restaurant, you can return whatever you don't like. Take a moment and say, "Excuse me God, this is not what I asked for. This is not what I wanted. Let me make it clear to you what I want." Then sit back, relax, and just as in a restaurant, allow it to come to you. Yes, there is a bill to pay. You must be willing to pay a price for whatever you want. That price may be time, money, energy or effort. Before you ask for something, make sure that you are willing to pay the bill when it comes. Don't set your expectations so high that nothing— no matter what you receive in life—will satisfy you.

My friend George went around the world looking for his perfect mate. He traveled high and low, east and west, searching for his beautiful, perfect wife. Soon he found himself in a small village in Italy where he came across a maiden fit for a king. She was beautiful and enchanting, an incredible lover and exquisite cook. However, her one flaw was that she snored. Soon the man left her and continued to search for the perfect wife. After a few months, he met a young woman in India. She was voluptuous, seductive, intelligent and fun to be with. Yet, her one flaw was that she liked coffee; he hated coffee. So, again he left her in search of that one perfect wife. After more months of searching, he found himself in Fairfield, Iowa. Had George finally found the perfect wife in, of all places, Iowa? She was drop-dead gorgeous and the best lover that he had ever been with. She was intelligent, witty, and a joy to be around. She was an incredible cook and made him feel wanted. Best of all, she didn't snore or drink coffee. Finally, after three years of searching all over the world, he had found his one perfect bride.

Last week, I received a phone call from George, who informed me that his perfect mate had left him. He was completely devastated. I asked him, "How could this possibly be? I thought that everything was perfect between you two?"

"So, did I," he sobbed. "Then she informed me that she was looking for the perfect man." I think that you get the moral of the story. So, in conclusion, ask, be worthy, set realistic expectations, and KNOW that it has already been given to you.

Chapter Six

The Matrix of Your Dreams

There is no greater opportunity to reach the matrix of God than through dreams. Our dreams tell us where our shadow is and what it is trying to show us. When we heal and integrate our shadow self, the matrix of the dreamworld reflects that change. In this matrix, we open to what is possible in our lives and in our world. As you become more aware of the consciousness and awareness conveyed to you by your dreams, you will be able to manifest that in the matrix of reality.

Have you ever dreamed about being in a relationship, but in the dream your current relationship is taking place in your childhood home? This means that you are relating to this person the same way you related to people as a child.

Do you ever dream that you are in a car, but another person is driving? Pay close attention to who is driving. Is it your mother, father, or a past lover? This dream is saying that you are allowing that person to control and direct your life.

Have you ever dreamed that you were driving a car but couldn't put on the brakes? This is telling you that your life is out of balance and control. You need to take control of your life, so to speak.

Have you ever dreamed that the car that you were driving was going in reverse? This means you that you are going backwards in your life and need to shift gears.

Have you ever dreamed that the car that you were driving falls apart and the only thing left is the steering wheel? This dream is saying that you are falling apart or that you don't feel safe or protected.

Have you ever dreamed that your car engine was overheating? This dream is telling you that you are burned out or suffering from nervous exhaustion. So, stop, get a different job, and learn to relax.

Have you ever dreamed that you and your current partner are in the back seat of a car driven by the parents of one or the other of you? This means that your current relationship is based on the model left by the parents who are in the front seat.

Do you dream that you are your current age but still sleeping in your childhood bed? This may be an indication that you emotionally are still at home, thinking that others are responsible for you. It may also mean that the only way that you feel safe and protected is when you are close to home or your mother.

Do you ever dream that you are on an elevator or a spiral staircase going upwards? This is telling you that you are accessing your higher self and should pay attention. Should you become conscious of this dream while you are dreaming it, stop and ask a question.

On the other hand, have you ever dreamed that you were on an elevator or staircase and going downwards? This means that you are going into your subconscious, where a fear or an issue needs to be addressed. Again, if you become conscious of the dream while you are dreaming, stop and ask, "What is my fear?"

Do you dream that you are running? This means you are running from yourself. If so, STOP! Stop running, turn around and begin chasing. Make the fear afraid of you.

Have you ever dreamed that someone was knocking at your door but you were afraid to open it? This means that something is trying to become conscious. Pay close attention to where the door is at. Are you back in the place where you grew up? This is often a clue as to what your subconscious is trying to reveal.

Do you dream in color or black and white? If you have a dream in black and white, or if the dream seems to have a lot of shadows around it, there is a fear, and it is not based in truth. If it is in vivid color, it could be prophetic.

Have you ever dreamed that you looked at yourself in the mirror? Did you notice that your face may have began to contort and become almost evil in appearance? This indicates that you are perceiving yourself in unhealthy ways; your self-perception is distorted.

Have you dreamed you were in a relationship but your vision blurred in the dream? This dream is telling you that you are not seeing the situation at hand clearly.

Do you dream you are drowning? This dream is saying that your emotional body is drowning you. This usually relates to depression.

Have you dreamed that you were in a bakery and you could not stop eating sweets? This means you are eating too much sugar.

Do you dream that you are losing your teeth? This dream is telling you that you are insecure about something, or that you are insecure overall.

Have you ever dreamed that you were chewing bubble gum and the gum kept growing? This means you are afraid to ask for what you want.

Have you ever dreamed that you were grinding your teeth? This means that something is eating away at you.

Have you ever dreamed that you were looking at tornadoes coming towards you? Tornadoes often represent an inner conflict you need to look at. If you become conscious of the dream while you are dreaming, ask the tornadoes to reveal themselves to you.

Do you ever dream that you are in a palace, going in and out of numerous doors? This means you are going in circles looking for what you want. It could be trying to tell you to stop searching and go within.

Have you ever dreamed you were exercising with someone you are currently fighting with? This dream is telling you to work things out with them, and what it is you need to work out.

Have you ever dreamed that you were wrestling with someone? This means you are wrestling with yourself over someone or something. The same is true if you dream you are fighting with someone. This is reflecting your own inner struggles back to you.

Do you dream that you are trying to get on the airplane, but no matter how you try, you can't find the way to the airport? This dream is saying that you feel lost and have no direction in life.

Have you ever dreamed that you started to say something, but no words came out? This means you are afraid to speak up for yourself and ask for what you want. This dream could also be telling you that you feel misunderstood and not listened to by others. Pay attention to this type of dream if, in the dream, you are on the phone calling 911 and the cry for help does not come out of your mouth.

Have you ever dreamed that you were losing your hair? This reflects your own insecurities.

Have you ever dreamed that a love from the past is coming back to you, even though you know that this is impossible? This dream is saying that someone from your past will come into your life. You may get a letter or receive a phone call from that person, or he or she may actually come back into your life.

Whatever you dream, it is possible that the matrix of God is showing you what you need to work on. The good news is that the reverse is also true. Whatever you need to work on in your life can be healed in the matrix of your dreams.

Do you recall being attracted to someone when you were in high school? No matter how hard you tried, no matter what you did or said, that person completely ignored you. The more you were ignored, the more you tried to get his attention, thinking that you weren't doing enough to please him. Eventually, with a broken heart, you gave up and realized that the person you were attracted to was not interested in you.

How many years have you carried those feelings of hurt and resentment within while wondering "what if"? Well, now you can find out why she didn't open up to you. Before you go to sleep at night, ask that person to visit you in a dream and tell you why he didn't open up to you. Ask why she left you. Ask about the agreement the two of you made before you came here. Ask what was it that he needed to hear from you.

This technique can be applied to anything missing in your life. Ask your dreams to reveal the following: "What decision do I need to make to create _____ ? What needs to happen so that this can manifest? What decision am I making that continues to create pain in my life? What is it that I need energetically to heal myself?"

You can also use the matrix of your dreams to ask people you need to forgive—those who have passed on—to visit you in your dreams so you can express forgiveness. If you cannot forgive another who is in your life today, ask that individual's soul to come to you in a dream and create a space where you can forgive each other. You will be amazed at the results. Someone you have hated for years may even call you after visiting you in your dreams. Ask that, in your dreams, you heal your relationships with parents, children, or anyone who has violated you in the past. There is nothing that cannot be healed if there is a willingness to do so. Love will show you the way; you just have to be willing and allow it to take place.

All things, no matter how big or small, can be healed in the matrix of your dreams. The brother you lost as a child can return to you in your dreams. If you were adopted, you can ask that your biological parents come to you in a dream and explain why they couldn't handle the responsibility of a child. If you are attracted to someone, you can ask to see the agreement or contract that was made between you before you get serious in the relationship.

I think if you are attracted to someone, turning that relationship and or attraction over to God is very dangerous. In fact, it is dangerous to turn anything over to God. Rather, turn things over to your inner being, your higher self. Whatever the situation, it is best to simply say, "I surrender," and ask your inner knowing to reveal what you are longing to know. "We place ourselves in the most amount of trouble when we begin to think that anyone or anything outside of ourselves can save us," writes Ken Page, author of *The Way it Works*.

If you are thinking about relocating, ask your dreams to show you what your life will be like if you move to that particular city.

If you carry guilt about making a "bad" decision in the past, you can ask that the people hurt by your decision come to you in your dreams and forgive you.

Did you decide to abort a child? You can ask the soul of the unborn child to visit you in a dream and let you know that it is okay, and understood your decision.

Whatever you need can be received in the matrix of your dreams. This is an incredible tool that can help you heal all aspects of yourself. Use it and trust that works.

Chapter Seven

The Matrix of Sexuality

"When we have restored the sexual experience to the realm of the sacred, our world will be chaste, divine, holy and healed," says Deepak Chopra, M.D. I cannot think of anything that needs healing more than our own sexuality. Why is there so much confusion around sexuality? Why do we have sexually transmitted diseases? Why have we been taught that sexuality is bad, dirty, and sinful, yet it feels so good? What about masturbation? I haven't gone blind or developed hair on my palms, and it always feels good. If sexuality is innate and that desire comes from deep within, how can it be bad or shameful? If it comes from within, how can a gay or lesbian individual be immoral or wrong? How can homosexuality be a genetic defect?

From the point of view of genetics, we are all bi-sexual. Recently, science has shown that half of our genes are received from the male and half from the female. Why is it that if two beautiful, curvaceous women make love, society says it's okay? Yet if two attractive men have sex, that same society turns around and utters its disgust?

In a recent study I conducted at New Mexico State University, nearly 70 percent of the male respondents admitted that they were sexually aroused when they saw a well-endowed male in an adult movie. (For this survey, we defined well-endowed as 8 inches or more.)

Why is it that when a man sleeps with hundreds of women, he is called a stud? Yet if a female sleeps with hundreds of men, she is called a slut or a whore? Does the act of sex in and of itself cause disease, or are there other factors?

Finally, what can we do to heal the matrix of sex? What can we do to restore the sexual experience to the realm of the sacred and divine? What if the purpose of the orgasm is to help you connect directly into GOD?

French philosopher and mathematician Rene Descartes argued that consciousness was contained within the pineal gland. The pineal glad is an endocrine gland that is smaller than a quarter and located directly behind the center of your forehead. It is often referred to as the "master gland." I believe that if the pineal glad is activated directly, it will lead to altered states of consciousness, enabling you to become like the Christ. There is no greater way to activate Christ-Consciousness then by activating the pineal gland via an orgasm.

In Sanskrit, the ancient language of India, the word "chakra" refers to energy centers, or vortexes, in the body. These wheels of energy are located within the etheric body and relate to various functions of consciousness.

There are seven chakras. The first chakra—the root chakra—is located at the base of your spine. It is red in color and relates to sexuality and the sense of survival. The next chakra is the spleen chakra. Its color is orange and it relates to mobility in life. It is located between your genitalia and your navel. Third is the solar plexus chakra. Its color is yellow and it relates to your feelings and emotions. It is located in the center of your navel. Fourth is your heart chakra. Its color is green and it relates to your ability to love yourself and others. It is located at the level of your heart. Fifth is your throat chakra. Its color is blue and it relates to your ability to com- municate your ideas to the world. This is your center for self-expression. It is located at your adam's apple. Sixth is your third-eye chakra. Its color is indigo and it relates to your intuition and ability to trust yourself. It is located in the center of your forehead. Seventh is the crown chakra. Its color is a white and purple mixture; it relates to your God self or Higher self. This chakra is located at the top of your head.

When these wheels of energy are energized and balanced, you will feel energized and charged with vitality. When they are blocked due to emotionally charged imprints, they can cause illness and disease. So, what do these chakras have to do with sex, orgasm, the pineal gland, and the ability to achieve Christ-consciousness? In one word, everything.

How many of you have taken the time to notice from the inside what happens when you have an orgasm? Have you ever taken the time to follow the energy of the orgasm as it goes through the body? Or has it become just a release of pent up energy for you? I would guess that most people are not conscious of the energy that flows from within the body when having an orgasm. What if the orgasm's purpose is to flow upward into the chakra centers and activate the pineal gland, to the point that you would become one with God?

In Tantric sex, the male is taught to reverse the flow of his semen prior to climax and move it up through the energy centers, or chakras, until it reaches the pineal gland. With enough practice, a man can eventually achieve complete control of his ejaculation and orgasm so that it becomes an energizing experience, rather than a release which drains his vitality. If you pay close attention to the flow of the energy released in your body after you orgasm, notice where the flow stops. Does it go all of the way to the top of your head? I would guess that for most of you, it stops somewhere between your navel and your throat chakra. When your chakras are energized and balanced, they act like conductors of energy in the body, enabling the orgasm to travel directly into the pineal gland. Unfortunately, most of our guilt, fear, and shame is placed right between our legs. The vital energy only reaches the solar plexus or navel area in the body.

Now, let's stop and put two and two together. If you knew that sexuality was a key to achieving Christ or God consciousness, if you wanted to control the masses so that only one could be God, what better way to do so than to tell the masses that sexuality was sinful. In my opinion, this is why the church continues to profess that sexuality is shameful and bad. If sex is a key to becoming Christ-like, then sex becomes a threat to the power held by the church. If the orgasm could be used to develop your inner Christ, you wouldn't need the church's savior, teachings or dogmas. You wouldn't need the church at all. That is exactly why the church has gone to great lengths to suppress sexuality.

The Catholic Church went to such an extent to suppress sexuality that it refers to Mary as a virgin. Yet 2,000, years ago in the Middle East, the term "virgin" did not mean "not having sexual experience." It meant "not being attached to any man." The term was quite often reserved for temple prostitutes who initiated young males into adulthood. It is interesting to note that 2,000 years ago in the Middle East, a young woman was often referred to as a "virgo." Don't you think that it is quite possible that the term "virgo" got translated into "virgin"? I certainly do.

Your sexuality and ability to orgasm is your vehicle to becoming one with God. Why does the church make sexuality so sinful? Why does the church make homosexuality wrong? Why does the church make sex so shameful? What is the reason behind this suppression? Why does the church claim that the sole reason for sexuality is procreation? There can be only one reason—to keep you from remembering who you really are.

So, when you have sex with someone, make it sacred. Make it a ritual for the soul. Take the time to invoke the inner Christ, the light that is within each of you. Take the time to light candles and honor each other. Take the time to gaze deeply into each other's eyes and connect with each other's souls. Make kissing such a powerful act that it becomes more erotic than the act of sex itself. Touch. Take the time to touch, hold and caress.

It is really sad that in today's society, we only know two types of touch-ing—sexual and violence. When you hold and touch your partner, do it with love. Allow love to flow from your soul out to your finger tips. Allow your touch to become soft, gentle and nurturing. When you touch your partner, look at her and tell her you love her. Be willing to work with the body's energy centers and allow the sexual pulse to flow into each of the chakras and up towards the pineal gland. Allow the experience of orgasm to enter the realm of the sacred once again.

Until we do this, we will create more sexually transmitted diseases. So, let's look at what I think is the emotional cause behind most of these diseases, including HIV/AIDS. When I use the word "they," I am addressing human beings in general.

1) "Victim Consciousness." People feel helpless, powerless and defenseless.2) They feel that their bodies are not safe. They feel they are not protected in their bodies, or that they are not able to protect themselves.3) They despise themselves for being sexual and or gay.4) They experience tremendous guilt about sleeping with their best friend's wife or husband.

5) They lack the self esteem needed to say no when they don't want to have sex with someone. They say yes so they don't disappoint the other person, and then resent themselves for the sexual act.6) They were sexually violated as a child and learned that the only way they mattered was through their sexuality. In other words, they feel they can only receive love or attention because they are sexual. Or, because of this violation, they feel unable to defend themselves; they feel emotionally defenseless.7) They use sexuality to manipulate or hold power over others.

Does this help you understand that we have an emotional body that determines our health, more so than our physical body? Energy doesn't die, it only transforms. Therefore, the imprint of the violation remains in the body until it is released in a healthy way. This imprint has a consciousness that robs you of your life force and influences your behavior. The good news is that if what I am saying is true, healing your emotional body will also heal the physical symptoms. As Robin Williams said in the movie "Patch Adams," "If you treat an illness you may win or loose, if you treat the person, you will win every time, regardless of outcome." I think that most of us have a 5-year-old inside who calls the shots until we address, confront, and heal these emotional imprints. As we heal the imprints, we learn to use our sexuality, or orgasm, to discover who we really are. I think that GOD's purpose, when SHE gave us physical bodies, was to use sexuality and orgasm to become conscious co-creators.

Chapter Eight

The Imprint of HIV/AIDS

I believe it is the conflict between what society says is morally wrong and the feelings of joy during the sexual experience—combined with feelings of guilt and shame after the experience—that create sexually transmitted diseases, rather than the act of sex itself. To claim that homosexuals are more promiscuous than heterosexuals is erroneous. I find it hard to believe that homosexuals are more promiscuous than heterosexuals. If anything, the opposite would be true. It is foolish to state that homosexuals have a higher rate of HIV/AIDS then heterosexuals due to their promiscuity. I would guess that the reason why HIV/AIDS has affected far more homosexuals than heterosexuals is due to the discord within people who are gay. Who they are conflicts with what our society states is morally wrong. It is this inner turmoil, this conflict, this fear of not being accepted, that leads to the disease. Certainly, it is not created just by being gay. I believe it is created by the emotional conflict that gay people experience when they believe that they have to remain in hiding from society.

HIV doesn't discriminate. That may be true, but if you look at the demographics of HIV/AIDS, it appears that it does. There are currently 33.6 million people in the world who are infected with HIV/AIDS. Twenty-eight million of those are in Africa. Ninety-two percent of the 900,000 people living in America who are infected with HIV/AIDS are gay.

Here is a copy of an open letter that is on my web site at *http://www.angelfire.com/nm/mesmer* which I also sent to Senator Tom

Harkin of Iowa. (Senator Tom Harkin is a big supporter of nutritional supplements and has taken a strong stand against the FDA and AMA in their attempts to regulate vitamin and nutritional supplements.)

Dear Senator Tom Harkin:

I am not really an AIDS activist. I am more a part of the "Rethinking AIDS" movement and have a non-for profit organization called The Namaste.Org Our goal is to educate people on "New Choices for Healing Ourselves."

Dr. Jon Kaiser is a medical doctor in San Francisco, California. He has been on "Oprah" and "Good Morning America." He is the most successful western doctor treating HIV and AIDS. He has shown that HIV does not cause AIDS and that it can be completely reversed. Dr. Kaiser has the largest HIV/AIDS clinic in the world. Medicaid and Medicare (a.k.a. "We Don't Care") have shut his clinic down. His book, *Healing HIV*, has been deleted by the same people. Now, you can only get his book at *http://www.jonkaiser.com*

The hard, cold fact is that one-fifth of our nation's economy comes directly from the medical field. The largest contributors to Washington D.C.—even larger than all of the tobacco companies combined—are the pharmaceutical companies. I'll allow you to put two and two together and draw your own conclusions. A few years ago, our government admitted to injecting numerous black males in the military with Syphilis in 1952.

The average prescription drug is a ratio of 14:1 higher cost than the identical drug available in Canada and Mexico. Doctors in Australia are curing people with HIV/AIDS in 10 to 14 days by doing the following: They inject the blood of a person who is HIV+ into a horse, because horses are immune to the virus. They wait up to 72 hours, then withdraw the blood from the horse and extract the horse's antibodies. They inject the horse's antibodies into the HIV+ person. In three days, the virus stops growing and in 10 to 14 days, it is completely removed from the body. This is the same thing they did with the vaccine for polio, except they used blood from chickens rather than horses.

There are 33.6 Million HIV+ people in the world today. Twenty-eight million are in Africa, 900,000 in the U.S. and only 12,000 in Australia. Ninety-two percent of people with HIV in the U.S. are gay. Whoever created it did not like gays or blacks. There are speculations that in 1978, 1,000 monogamous gay males were injected with HIV in the San Francisco area via a hepatitis B vaccine. Dr. Ronald Strickland, Ret., U.S. Air Force, makes references to this in the "Strickland Document." This was also referred to in the HBO movie, "And the Band Played On" (Please note: the following is taken from Waves Forrest.)

Despite repeated denials from Defense Department officials, allegations persist that AIDS is a genetically altered virus which has been deliberately released to wipe out homosexuals and/or non-whites in the U.S., and to reduce populations in third-world countries.

At first glance, it seems like the epitome of paranoia to accuse the military of conspiring to exterminate citizens of its own country, including some of its own troops. However, the vast majority of military personnel could be completely unaware of such a plot in their midst, while a relative handful of traitors in key positions could conduct it under cover of classified operations. The circumstantial evidence is actually quite compelling: the AIDS virus was artificially engineered and planted in several different locations at about the same time through vaccination programs and, possibly, blood bank contamination.

At a House Appropriations hearing in 1969, the Defense Department's Biological Warfare (BW) division requested funds to develop, through gene-splicing, a new disease that would both resist and break down a victim's immune system. "Within the next five to 10 years, it would probably be possible to make a new infective micro-organism which could differ in certain important respects from any known disease-causing organisms. Most important of these is that it might be refractory to the immunological and therapeutic processes upon which we depend to maintain our relative freedom from infectious diseases." (See—*A Higher Form of Killing: The Secret Story of Chemical and Biological Warfare*, by R. Harris and J. Paxman, p 266, Hill and Wang, pub.) The funds were approved. AIDS appeared within the requested time frame and has the exact characteristics specified.

In 1972, the World Health Organization published a similar proposal: "An attempt should be made to ascertain whether viruses can in fact exert selective effects on immune function, e.g., by…affecting T cell function as opposed to B cell function. The possibility should also be looked into that the immune response to the virus itself may be impaired if the infecting virus damages more or less selectively the cells responding to the viral antigens." ("Bulletin of the W.H.O.", vol. 47, p 257- 274.) This is a clinical description of the function of the AIDS virus.

The incidence of AIDS infections in Africa coincides exactly with the locations of the W.H.O. smallpox vaccination program in the mid-1970s. *(London Times*, May 11, 1987) Some 14,000 Haitians then on UN secondment to Central Africa were also vaccinated in this campaign. Personnel actually conducting the vaccinations may have been completely unaware that the vaccine was anything other than what they were told.

A striking feature of AIDS is that it is ethno-selective. The rate of infection is twice as high among Blacks, Latinos and Native Americans as among whites, with death coming two to three times as swiftly. And over 80 percent of children with AIDS and 90 percent of infants born with it are among these minorities. "Ethnic weapons" that would strike certain racial groups more heavily than others have been a long-standing U.S. Army BW objective. (Harris and Paxman, p 265)

Under the current U.S. administration, biological warfare research spending has increased 500 percent, primarily in the area of genetic engineering of new disease organisms.

The "discovery" of the AIDS virus (HTLV3) was announced by Dr. Robert Gallo at the National Cancer Institute, which is on the grounds of Fort Detrick, Maryland, a primary U.S. Army biological warfare research facility. Actually, the AIDS virus looks and acts much more like a cross between a bovine leukemia virus and a sheep visna (brain-rot) virus, cultured in a human cell culture, than any virus of the HTLV group.

The closest thing in this case to a "smoking test tube" so far is the AIDS virus itself. If it was possible for such a monstrosity to occur naturally, it would have done so ages ago and decimated mankind at that time. Some other life form would presently be in control of this planet (assuming that is not already the case).

The Hepatitis B vaccine study in 1978 appears to have been the initial means of planting the infection in New York City. The test protocol specified non-monogamous males only, and homosexuals received a different vaccine from heterosexuals. At least 25 to 50 percent of the first reported New York AIDS cases in 1981 had received the Hepatitis B test vaccine in 1978. By 1984, 64 percent of the vaccine recipients had AIDS, and the figures on the current infection rate for the participants of that study are held by the U.S. Department of Justice, and are unavailable.

The AIDS epidemic emerged full-blown in the three U.S. cities with organized gay communities before being reported elsewhere, including Haiti or Africa, so it is epidemiologically impossible for either of those countries to be the origin point for the U.S. infections.

Another indication that AIDS had multiple origin points is that the 14-month doubling time of the disease cannot nearly account for the current number of cases if we assume only a small number of initial infections starting in the late 1970s.

Before dismissing the possibility that a U.S. Army BW facility would participate in genocide, bear in mind that hundreds of top Nazis were imported into key positions in the U.S. military- intelligence establishment following WW II. U.S. military priorities were then re-oriented from defeating Nazis to defeating communism at any cost, and strengthening military control of economic and foreign policy decisions (See—"Project Paperclip" by Clarence Lasby, Atheneum 214, NY, and *Gehlen: Spy of the Century*, by E.H. Cookridge, Random House.) There's no proof those Nazis ever gave up their long-term goals of conquest and genocide just because they changed countries. Fascism was and is an international phenomenon.

It's not as if this was total reversal of previous U.S. military policy. However. Hitler claimed to have gotten his inspiration for the "final solution" from the extermination of Native Americans in the U.S. For that matter, the first example of germ warfare in the U.S. was in 1763 when some of the European colonists gave friendly Indians a number of blankets that had been infected with smallpox, causing many deaths.

One indication of the actual U.S. military priorities regarding BW was the importation of the entire Japanese germ warfare unit (#731) following WW II. These people killed over 3,000 POWs, including many Americans, in a variety of grisly experiments, yet they were granted complete amnesty and given American military positions in exchange for sharing their research findings with their U.S. Army counterparts.

Consider also the callous attitude displayed by top military officials toward veterans suffering from the after-effects of exposure to Agent Orange and radiation from nuclear weapons' tests.

In fact, since the end of WW II, over 200 experimental BW tests have been conducted on civilians and military personnel in the U.S. One example was the test spraying from Sept. 20-26, 1950, of bacillus globigi and syraceus maracezens over 117 square miles of the San Francisco area, causing pneumonia-like infections in many of the residents. The family of one elderly man who died in the test sued the government, but lost. To this day, syraceus is a leading cause of death among the elderly in the San Francisco area. Another case was the joint Army-CIA BW test in 1955, still classified, in which an undisclosed bacteria was released in the Tampa Bay region of Florida, causing a dramatic increase in whooping cough infections, including 12 deaths. A third example was the July 7-10, 1966 release of bacteria throughout the New York subway system, conducted by the U.S. Army's Special Operations Division. Due to the vast number of people exposed, it would be virtually impossible to identify, let alone prove, any specific health problems resulting directly from this test.

Despite the loyalty of the vast majority of U.S. military personnel toward their country, there are clearly some military officials who have very different intentions. They occupy high enough positions to impose their priorities on military programs and get away with it, so far.

The first detailed charges regarding AIDS as a BW weapon were published in the Patriot, a newspaper in New Delhi, India, on July 4, 1984. It is hard to say where the investigations of this story in the Indian press might have led if they had not been sidetracked by two major domestic disasters shortly thereafter: the assassination of Indira Gandhi on October 31 and the Bhopal Union Carbide plant "accident" that killed several thousand and injured over 200,000 on December 3.

The Soviet press picked up the story in October 1985, making it easy for U.S. Defense Department spokesmen to dismiss the charges as Soviet propaganda, even though many other countries carried it. The Soviets recently retracted the charges, in the new spirit of US-USSR cooperation.

A variation on the AIDS-BW theory that is popular in far-right publications is that AIDS was developed in Soviet laboratories for use against the U.S. An obvious problem with this idea is that the victims of choice of a Soviet BW attack would be anti-communists, not minorities or homosexuals, who are generally more left-wing. The people at greatest risk from AIDS in the U.S. are in fact the very elements most disliked by arch-conservatives. In any case, it is simplistic to assume that one country, the U.S. or USSR, is conducting this campaign against one another. Although concealed in apparent conflicts between nations, the real culprits are multi-national fascists on both sides, still bent on massive population reductions and global domination.

Other motives include the old "divide and conquer" principle. AIDS is inspiring fear and mistrust among people, and scaring them away from relating to each other sexually. It is acting as a barrier to the attempted cultural resurgence toward peace, love and cooperation. Of high school students surveyed last year as to which decade they'd most like to have grown up in, 90 percent chose the 60s. The last thing pro-war fascists want is another love generation, especially if it is more politically sophisticated than the last one.

Apparently, homosexuals were an initial target in the U.S. because their sexual practices would help in the rapid spread of the disease, and because it was correctly assumed that very few non-homosexual citizens would pay much attention during the early years of the epidemic. Also, the stigma of a "homosexual disease" would interfere with rational analysis and discussion of AIDS. Bear in mind that homosexuals were among the first to be exterminated in Nazi Germany, before Jews or other minorities, so fewer citizens would object.

The details of precisely how the AIDS virus was synthesized, mass-cultured, and spread by incorporating it into vaccination programs are available but fairly intricate. It is beyond the scope of this report to present a crash course in virology, epidemiology, genetic engineering, and the military strategies of international fascism. Readers are encouraged to obtain and study the references cited here, and to demand a full inquiry. Those officials who are actually involved in the coverup will reveal this by their inaction when pressed to investigate.

Evil is hard to confront, especially on the preposterous scale we have here. If you acknowledge the presence of those who think their only hope for survival is to kill off two-thirds of all the other kinds, and their ability to manage such an act, you pretty much have to do something about it.

I seriously doubt that HIV causes AIDS. AZT was banned from medical practice in 1963 because it inhibits the body's production of white blood cells. Any virus that goes into the blood stream will result in an HIV+ test. Several leaders in the field of alternative medicine can prove that 60 illnesses can show up in the result of an HIV+ test, including the flu. Any virus that goes into the blood stream will result in an HIV+ test.

In 1997, an episode of the "X-Files" aired in which Agent Molder contracted a retro-virus. Other characters in the show withdrew his blood, raised his blood temperature by five degrees, and injected it back into him. They then withdrew the blood again, lowered it by five degrees, and repeated the process. This raising and lowering of the blood's temperature is done in the United Kingdom. The result: AIDS deaths in the United Kingdom have dropped between 80 and 90 percent since 1997. Yes, Hollywood showed the world how to cure AIDS and no one got it.

PLEASE, call Medicare/Medicaid and scream about this. Call your local congress person, as NO ONE needs to die from HIV/AIDS any more. You are either part of the problem or part of the solution. If more people go the alternative route, then HIV/AIDS will become a thing of the past. (It will happen.) It is happening; it is already done.

Even AIDS activists now realize that people infected with HIV are dying from AZT, not HIV. (Again, AZT was banned in 1963 by the medical community because it inhibits the body's production of white blood cells.) This makes me mad, quite frankly. So please, let's end the AIDS "experiment." Together, we can make it happen.

If you think this is crap, read the book *Inventing the AIDS Virus*, by Dr. Peter Duesberg. His information is quite remarkable. He is a world-renowned retro virus expert at UCLA in Berkeley, California, whose work is being confirmed by two different Nobel prize winners. You can also obtain Gary Null's information. He is successfully treating people with HIV/AIDS by giving them 25,000 mg of vitamin C a day. He was probably one of the first people to openly criticize the AMA for treating HIV with AZT. His documentary video, *"Power, Profits, and Politics of AIDS,"* is an eye opener.

In 1996, Bob Guiccione, the editor of "Penthouse," launched a $200 billion class action suit against the AMA and the National Cancer Society for deliberately altering the effectiveness of Hydrazine Sulfate in treating cancer. Hydrazine Sulfate has been shown to cure most forms of cancer within 30 to 90 days, and it only cost $30 for a month's supply. Unfortunately, the medical establishment instructed patients to take barbiturates along with the Hydrazine Sulfate. When taken together, the barbiturates made the Hydrazine Sulfate null and void. In early 1997, this lawsuit was featured on the Montel Williams talk show but since then, it has been placed under a gag rule. At $30.00 a month, do you realize how this would effect our nation's economy? People, wake up!

Again, the more people who know about this, the sooner this cure for HIV/AIDS and cancer will be available. It is now being suppressed. What is even more scary is that if Dr. Peter Duesberg is correct, the hypothesis that HIV is the cause of AIDS has been completely fabricated. There are others who are taking his claim one step further—HIV may not exist at all. You will find more information on this by visiting the web sites listed below.

http://www.nexusmagazine.com/HIVnotAIDS1.html
http://www.nexusmagazine.com/HIVnotAIDS2.html
http://www.nexusmagazine.com/HIVnotAIDS3.html
http://www.nexusmagazine.com/irt1.html
http://www.nexusmagazine.com/irt2.html
http://www.nexusmagazine.com/chachoua.html

If you would like to transform the quality of life on this planet and give the ability to heal back to the patient, I need your support. Your contribution of $50 or more is fully tax- deductible. In return, you will receive a monthly newsletter filled with the latest information on what works and doesn't work in the field of alternative medicine. One newsletter could possibly save you thousands of dollars in medical costs. It could also prevent you from being one of the 98,000-148,000 people who die from "medical errors" each year. The newsletter will also feature up-to-date legislative news about laws that effecting alternative health care. Together, we can keep the FDA and the AMA from regulating holistic health care, alternative medicine, and your right to vitamin/herbal supplements. Let's take back our health and put an end to the suppression of cures for disease in the name of big money.

You may send a money order payable to The Namaste.Org Amounts under $250 do not require an invoice. Should your generosity exceed $250, you will receive an invoice. Send your money orders to:

> Namaste.Org
> c/o Mark Patterson
> P.O. Box 384
> La Mesa, NM 88044

Namaste, Mark Patterson

I have purposely chosen not to cite the sources of the information given above or below. Why? Because I want you, the reader, to do your own research on HIV/AIDS. Again, I am not asking you to believe in anything I am stating here. I want you to find out for yourself. In my opinion, HIV/AIDS was initially an attempt to engineer population control that has now become a marketing tool to keep people afraid of their own sexuality and of each other. (However, much of the information was taken from *USA Today*; *U.S. News and World Report*; the *Las Cruces Sun News*; President Bill Clinton, who has voiced his concern about medical errors; the book *Inventing the AIDS Virus* by Dr. Peter Duesberg; the book *The Ancient Secret of the Flower of Life* by Drunvalo Melchizedek and his Flower of Life Workshops; the book *Conspiranoia* by John Drevold; Waves Forest author of AIDS Biological and Psychological Warefare, leading-edge alternative health expert and best-selling author; Gary Null; and finally, Lee Carroll, co-author of *The Indigo Children*. However, none of the cited information has come from the *National Inquirer*, *The Star*, or any other tabloid magazine. It is safe to say that you will be able to verify all of these statements as they have been made public within the past few years. I encourage you to do so.

In 1998, it was announced that the number of AIDS deaths in the U.S. had declined by 42 percent the previous year. This is absolutely unheard of regarding any disease known to man. From 1990-1992, numerous children were born infected with HIV/AIDS. In fact, some of them developed full-blown ARC and then miraculously, soon after, recovered completely with very little medical help. By the time these children were around 5 or 6 years old, there was no evidence to suggest that they were once HIV+. I believe these children are the children of the blue race.

Lee Carroll and Jan Tobler refer to these remarkable children as "Indigo children." They seem to know everything and are immune to HIV/AIDS. Most importantly, if these children can heal themselves of HIV/AIDS, then anyone can. Remember the matrix quality to life. These children have left an imprint in the human race's matrix that is an instruction on how to cure HIV/AIDS. In my opinion, this is the real reason there was a 42 percent decline in AIDS deaths in 1997. If you are HIV+, get the facts and look into alternative cures. Do not believe what the medical community professes to know about HIV/AIDS. Ask that the matrix of God reveal the decision you made that created the HIV/AIDS within you. Once you know this underlying cause, forgive yourself. Wisdom erases karma. Finally, ask that you receive the imprint of the cure for AIDS that the Indigo Children placed in the matrix of humanity and be healed. They are healing this matrix as of June 2000, New AIDS cases, even in the highest risk categories have dropped by 60 percent. "New AIDS cases have dropped from 100,000 a year, peaked in the mid to late eighties to 40,000, a year now." (Center for Disease Controls, Atlanta, GA)

Chapter Nine

Healing the Matrix of Sexuality

I think that the first thing we must do is to stop making sexuality wrong, bad. and sinful. The second thing we need to do is to stop making people who are gay and lesbian wrong, bad, and sinful. How can homosexuality be immoral? Things are only moral or immoral because a group of people agree to label them as such.

I am not convinced that the Bible is GOD's word. Rather, it is the word of inspired white men who claimed that everything in it is God's word. From this perspective, the Bible becomes the word of God according to Paul, Peter, Luke, Matthew, etc. However, during certain historical periods, people were persecuted if they didn't believe that the Bible was God's word. Yet if I make the same claim—that I am speaking directly to God—then I am considered an agent of evil. Do you see how the established church has placed a facade of power over the masses so that church officials could have access to God and you and I could not? During the Middle Ages, convincing people to convert to Christianity was rather simple. You either accepted Jesus as your savior or you were killed. (Well, of course you are going to accept Jesus as your savior, duh!) Millions of people have been killed throughout history because they were judged to be unclean by those who claim to be saved. I think that any TV evangelist who cries out about the persecution of today's Christians needs to take a long, hard look at history. "As you sow, so shall you reap." "What comes around, goes around."

Why is it that the religious right has gone out of its way to label homosexuality deviant? I think they missed the line in the Bible where Jesus said, "Judge no one, for you do not know how they stand in the eyes of God." I think they also forgot to realize that we all have souls. Souls have no gender, and it is the two souls who are attracted to each other. Attraction has no sex or gender. Love has no sex or gender; love is love. If there is a pure attraction and a love between two individuals of the same sex, how can that love be wrong, bad, or shameful? In numerous ancient cultures such as Lemuria, Sumeria, and even some of the Mayan and Aztec civilizations, homosexuals were worshiped and held in high esteem. Historical evidence also suggests that in ancient Egypt and Greece homosexuals were considered part of society's elite.

Finally, we need to stop making people who are infected with HIV/AIDS wrong, bad, and sinful. How ironic that the Catholic Church, which professed that AIDS was God's way of punishing gay people, is now admitting that a number of priests are dying from HIV/AIDS. Again, this is caused from the inner turmoil created when one's words and beliefs are in conflict with one's actions. Suppression of sexuality in the Catholic priesthood has led to sexual violations of choir boys, abortions, and now AIDS. Suppressed sexuality creates the discord that results in sexually transmitted diseases. Look at cultures where sexuality is openly and honestly expressed. In these cultures, sexually transmitted diseases are literally non-existent.

Sexuality is a gift from God, and the angels envy our ability to orgasm. The angels envy our ability to orgasm? Yes, that is correct. In fact, the next time you have sex, you may want to invite your angels and your higher self to participate in the sexual experience. With the higher frequencies of your higher self and the angels, the orgasm can open the door to new levels of consciousness. Love yourself for being sexual. God created you as a sexual being. Your sexuality is innate and comes from within. Therefore, it can only be good!

However, if you are addicted to sex, then take the time to acknowledge that addiction and discover its underlying causes. What feelings of loneliness and emptiness are you trying to fill through sex? As a teenager, did you learn that the only way you could receive love or attention was by being sexual? Did you learn that the only way to matter to another was by being sexual? Were you sexually violated as a child? These questions may provide the answer to the cause of your sexual addiction.

Currently, I am a guest columnist for "Big-Date," an adult web site created for those who like to explore all aspects of sexuality. I write the column to provide information that enables others to use sexuality as a tool for spiritual development. The column also enables others to drop their inhibitions about sexuality. To quote my angels, "Please remove guilt and shame from sexuality and let others who are exploring alternative lifestyles know that there is absolutely nothing wrong with it." Here are some questions from Big-Date members and answers written by me, taken from *http://www.big-date.com* (The following section contains subject matter than may not be appropriate for all audiences.)

Please note that I am not a licensed professional. These are my opinions. You, and you alone, are responsible for the advice I provide in this column. If you have serious concerns, please seek the help of a qualified professional.

I am a very attractive gay male with a 7.5 inch penis. Anytime that I am with another male who is bigger than me, I cannot achieve an erection. Why does this happen?

With 7.5 inches, you are already bigger that 75 percent of the male population. More often than not, when we measure and compare ourselves to other people, we come from a place of lack, meaning we feel that "I am not enough." When we come from a place of lack, we feel that we cannot satisfy the other partner. It is this fear of not being able to satisfy our partner that causes the inability to achieve an erection. This performance anxiety was at one time a huge issue for me. It kept me from having sex until I was 23. So, you may want to read Healing the Shame that Binds You by John Bradshaw, or see a hypnotherapist in your area and work on self-acceptance and self-love.

Hello Mark. I am 24 years old. I have a question for you, but first let me describe my problem. I found your web page and read that you are a gifted visionary. Please help me with my situation. I had sex with a girl one year ago and after that, I lost interest in women. It was my first sexual experience in life and I did not get any pleasure from having sex with that girl. I also did not get enough of an erection to achieve ejaculation. (I felt very tense and uncomfortable with her and also, I was embarrassed.) I got very disappointed about having sex with women, and after that day my desire for women disappeared (even though I was always interested in women before).

But the real problem is that I started to get strong erections when I saw naked men. The fantasy of having sex with a man comes to mind and I don't know how to get rid of it. Before having sex with that girl, I was always interested in women but after that, I lost interest in women and now have interest in men. I don't have any sexual relationships with men and had sex with a man only once. I did not like it and felt very guilty about doing it. Now, I keep thinking that sex with men is more pleasurable and exciting, and I keep getting erections when I see naked men. My question: Is it possible to get rid of this fantasy through hypnosis or do you think that I am homosexual? Is it possible to get an erection through hypnosis when I am with a woman?

First, thanks for taking the time to ask me these questions that concern you. I appreciate the fact that you chose me to help you. I love women; I love having sex with woman. However, I also get turned on by seeing a well-endowed male. I have often been curious about giving and receiving oral sex with another male. But that is it. I have no desire to have anal sex with a man. It doesn't turn me on at all. A close friend of mind, Guathemoch, a Mayan Astrologer, and numerous others have stated that as we evolve spiritually, we evolve sexually. This means that the more evolved we become, the more open we are to being bi-sexual. Eventually, we become asexual and learn how to reproduce from within.

I can assure you that when you die, God doesn't care if you are gay, bi-, or straight. God wants you to love yourself UNCONDITION-ALLY. The fact of the matter is, we are all BI-SEXUAL from a genetic point of view. Half of your genes are from the male and the other from the female. So, you are innately BI-SEXUAL. YES, you are GAY. Unfortunately, you want to label those feelings as "bad." You have desires that conflict with what society, religion, etc says is wrong. Did you ever stop to think that just because a group of people call something moral or immoral doesn't makes it moral or immoral? It is just what people have chosen to agree on. It doesn't mean that they are right.

Most of society's beliefs are based in fear, power and control. If you were to free yourself from the fear of being judged or condemned as being bad for your innate desires, you would be LIBERATED. You would experience FREEDOM. Once you are liberated, you become a threat to establishment. You begin to ask questions. You question authority and begin to say "I AM." I saw a bumper sticker the other day that said, "If you were really paying attention to what was going on, you would be outraged!"

There is a high price to pay for being a martyr to your own joy. It is simply not necessary. One of my mentors, Dick Sutphen, *http://www.dicksutphen.com,* tells a story about a man who always wanted to have sex with another male, but was afraid of being caught. He was afraid of all of the taboos that have been placed on the word "homosexual."

Finally, he gave in and had sex with another man. Guess what he discovered? He found, HAPPINESS...FREEDOM...PLEASURE. He freed himself from the chains of fear that had kept him bound in guilt and shame. "Homosexuality," "Heterosexuality," "Bi-Sexuality"— these are just labels society has agreed upon. You see, it is the two souls who are attracted to each other. The soul has no gender.

So, you and only you can make homosexuality wrong. Can you find some way in your heart to love yourself for being gay? Can you turn away from the teachings of society and listen to your own heart? Can you make it okay with yourself that you are gay?

By what I have read and seen, only a small amount of women have orgasms during intercourse. Is there anything that can be done for a woman to help her climax, at least during intercourse? Of course, it would be great if she did while her partner did, as well. Does the size of the man make a difference in terms of a woman being able to climax?

This is a great question and I think that I can help. First, take more time and slow down. Stop going directly for the big bang. Take the time to touch, caress and hold her. Take the time to make eye contact with her and gaze deeply into each other's souls. Kiss, kiss, and kiss. Make kissing so passionate that it becomes more incredible than the act of sex itself. Go down on her like there is no tomorrow... UNDERSTAND. Eat her pussy as if your life depends upon it. Do it PASSIONATELY! While you are eating her clit, finger fuck her pussy as well. You can reach around her buttocks and use your thumb, if you have too. Suck her toes and tickle her feet using feathers and massage oil, and then finger fuck her pussy super hard and fast while you are sucking her toes. Start with just one finger, then work your way into two and three. This will drive a woman wild. And try this: Make a "V" like shape with your right index finger and your right middle finger with your palm facing upward. Use your middle finger to fuck her pussy. As it goes in and out, allow your index finger to go up and down against her clit.

If a woman can handle it and if it doesn't make you climax too quickly, fuck her as hard and as fast as you can with everything that you've got. Wear a rubber if you climax too quickly. (An average male orgasms in 2 minutes, for females it usually takes 20 minutes) Spanking, biting, scratching and hair pulling can also be very erotic if not done too hard.

Allow a woman to play with her clit while you are fucking her. I know that some men feel inferior while she is doing this, and at first it is awkward, but that is crap. You are there to please her. If you do it doggie style, have her play with her clit at the same time and you will notice that her pussy becomes tighter; it feels really great. Allowing a woman to use her vibrator on her clit while you are fucking her can produce one of the most intense orgasms for a woman. It takes a bigger cock and some maneuvering on both parts, but it will drive her wild.

Finally, find out what makes her super hot and super horny, dripping wet, AND BE WILLING TO DO IT! Talk dirty to each other, talk to each other, tell her how you love to be inside of her. Let her know that she makes you super hard and hot. Find out what she wants to hear and say it. Let her know what you want to hear. Give your self permission to talk sexually while having sex. It is a great turn on for me to hear, "Damn, your cock is huge," "It is amazing what a difference an inch or two can make." "I want to suck that big cock of yours now."

Which brings us to the latter part of your question. It has become obvious to me that women are far more visual then we have been led to believe. Women are far more sexually aroused when they see a man who has a good, solid 8-9 inch thick cock. (However, anything bigger than 10 inches may scare them away.) If a woman is sexually aroused, she is more willing to drop her inhibitions, let go, and allow herself to have an orgasm. So, a bigger cock can make a difference in a woman's ability to achieve orgasm. (The average male is 6 inches when erect; the average location of the "g-spot" is 7 to 8 inches up inside a woman). So, a man with a larger penis can hit all of the HOT spots.)

Does size really matter? Well, in 1997, Durex Condoms did a study on that very question and they found that nearly 70 percent of the women who responded were unhappy with their partners' present size. So, I decided to do a similar study. Here are the results:

For my research and methods class at NMSU, I conducted a survey asking over 100 women, chosen at random, ages 18-40, eight questions related to the question, "Does size matter?" This was so random that I had five women say that they couldn't partake in the survey because they were still virgins. But, before we get to the results, I will give you some operational definitions of the survey and some of the background information that was given to the subjects.

I live in Las Cruces, New Mexico. It is about as multi-cultural as a city can get. Caucasians are the minority here. So, I think that the results of this study can be generalized to the larger population. In fact, I know that they can. You have my permission to quote this study or use it for a conversational piece at your next party. I think that you will find the results very interesting. The survey stated the following:

According to the Kinsey report on sexuality in America, the average male penis is 5.5 inches when erect. For this survey, we will define a large penis or larger penis as being at least 8 inches. Less than 2 percent of the entire male population has a penis size of 9 inches or more. A male is two times as likely to have an erect penis of 3.75 inches than one of 9 inches. I am only including six questions, and results that I think are most relevant and important to the readers of this book.

When asked the following:

(1) "Do you require a large penis (i.e., at least 8") to sexually satisfy you?" 35% replied YES, 65% replied NO.

2) "Are you more sexually aroused when you see a man with a large penis?" Nearly 90% replied YES, 10% replied NO.

3) "Have you ever wanted to have sex with a man with a larger penis?" Again, nearly 90% replied YES, 10% replied NO.

4) "Does having a Larger Penis make a man a better lover?" 35% said YES, 65% said NO.

5) "Have you ever ended an intimate relationship because a partner's penis was too small?"

Over 80% said YES!!!! less than 20 percent said NO.

This was the one response that we did not anticipate. It was a complete shock! However, it suggests that size really does matter.

6) "What is the ideal size or what size works best for you?" (On a scale of 3 to 12")

Again, over 80% said that the ideal size is 7 to 9," with 8" being the most frequently selected as being the ideal size. Only 20% said that 6" works best. No one said more than 9" Many women also noted that thickness or circumference was also important, the thicker the better.

Conclusion:

Is a larger penis required to sexually satisfy a woman? In general, no. The key word is REQUIRED. However, a larger penis MORE SEXU-ALLY AROUSES a woman and nearly every respondent has fantasized about or desired to be filled up with a well-endowed male.

Does size matter? Based on this study and my own experience, YES it does! We certainly were not expecting the high number of respondents who have ended an intimate relationship because a partner's penis was too small. Finally, as I have stated in my initial column on "Big-Date," most women do not require a larger penis but rather prefer 7 to 9 inches as the ideal size. Why? Because size does matter. A larger penis is more sexually arousing for a woman. Women in general are turned on by seeing a well-endowed male. (NOT HUGE ONES) Some are SO BIG that they can literally scare a woman away. The brain, after all, is the largest sex organ.

We also asked 100 men chosen at random ages 18 to 40 questions of a similar nature. Nearly 80 percent responded that, YES, women do prefer a penis of at least 8". Again, nearly 80 percent of those responded wanted and desired a larger penis. Finally, almost 90 percent said that they were 6 inches when fully erect. Most guys only have 6 inches and yet Most women want 7 to 9 inches. Does size matter? YOU BET!

(NMSU and the Psychology Department at NMSU did not condone or endorse the study I conducted on campus here in Las Cruces, New Mexico. I continued this study after being informed that the Psychology Department found it inappropriate.)

Now, don't get me wrong here guys. You are not just your dick. (No matter how hard you may want to believe that, there is far more to you then your dick) Women, after all, are not attracted to the phallus, but rather to the guy that the phallus is attached to. I know that many of you are wondering why I have included this information in a book about spirituality. Well, if I don't include this and my book takes off, someone out there is going to tell the press that I am a columnist for an adult web site, not to mention what the web site is about. So, later on in this book there will be a chapter entitled "The Matrix of Dr. Deeper," which will give you all of the details of the skeletons in my closet. Before ending this chapter, I would like to make a few comments about President Bill Clinton and Monica Lewinsky.

The truth is, there are no accidents or coincidences. President Bill Clinton and Monica Lewinsky agreed to participate in the current situation long before either one of them incarnated on Earth. These two souls have shared numerous lifetimes together and made a contract for this one with God. I don't think that anyone realizes the sacrifice these two individuals made in standing before this country on the issue of sexuality. Do you see now that they were merely teachers for all of us? They were reflecting back to us our own issues of sexuality, morals, and fidelity.

I am sure that your buttons got pushed when President Clinton admitted that he had inappropriate relations with Miss Lewinsky. I am sure that many of you felt he should have been removed from office due to his behavior. I am sorry, but lying about a blow job does not constitute removal from office. Do you really think that God would allow Republican hypocrites to pass judgement on the nation's leader and get away with it?

Unfortunately, we couldn't see the truth behind the drama. How we are addicted to drama. There is no greater addiction in society than our addiction too drama. We love drama, but then we turn around and complain that our life doesn't work. The truth is, President Clinton and Monica Lewinsky stood before this nation as teachers. They represented for all of us an area in which we have failed to show self-mastery time and time again. As mirrors, they stood naked before us and said, "Sexuality needs to be healed." If there is one area where we most need to heal, it is sexuality. Thank you Bill and Monica, thank you!

Chapter Ten

The Matrix of the Gift Behind All Things

If there is one question that I am asked more often then others when talking about my Near Death Experience, it is, "Why does God allow bad things to happen to good people?" The answer is that there are no victims, only volunteers. We all made agreements and contracts before we came here. Therefore, life is designed so that we can evolve. What we must realize is that there is a gift in all things—a truth, a lesson—that is presented regardless of the circumstance or situation.

When I look at the JonBenet Ramsey murder case, what amazes me is that no one has addressed the problem of placing children in beauty pageants. In my opinion, a 5-year-old girl should not be pressured to perform and dress like an adult. What is a 5-year-old girl doing on stage wearing make up and adult-type dresses? For that matter, why are 14 to 16-year-old girls doing the same thing? Why are we exploiting these children?

In my opinion, the parents of JonBenet Ramsey should be charged with child exploitation. I have heard the Ramseys say, "JonBenet wanted to do the pageants; she loved them." I am sorry, Mr and Mrs Ramsey, your argument is not logical. A child of that age has a difficult time discerning what pleases her and what pleases her parents. She longs to please her parents and constantly seeks their approval. In my opinion, she should have never been under that type of pressure. She was doing it to please her parents. We need to let children be children. Beauty pageants exploit young children for the gratification of their parents. Maybe this was the gift of

JonBenet Ramsey's death. Maybe her life's purpose was to get our attention, to expose the issue of exploiting children in these pageants. How much louder do you want God to scream at us? What more do you think God needs to do in order to get our attention?

Why are we allowing Michael Jordan to sell his shoes at $120 a pair while 12 to 14-year-old children in Malaysia make his shoes in sweat shops for $1 a day? What about Martha Stewart or other celebrities who exploit these children in the USA? What is it going to take for us to stop? How many more 6-year-old girls need to be shot in school in order to get us out of denial? How many more Susan Smiths need to drop their children into the lake before we stop violating and exploiting our children and other people's children? How many more teenagers will give birth at their proms and simply walk away from their newborn child, or leave it to die in the garbage? When are we going to wake up and acknowledge that there is a problem with violence among our young people? When are we going to put an end to the child abuse that has run rampant in America? What is it going to take?

Do you recall what you were doing when the verdict of the O.J. Simpson trial was announced? I was working at Vito's, a restaurant in Cedar Rapids, Iowa, and all across the nation, the reaction was the same. African Americans rejoiced in his victory while Caucasians were dismayed by the verdict. Despite the racial problems with the Los Angeles Police Department, the evidence overwhelmingly indicated that Simpson was the sole killer. Racial prejudice cannot alter genetics, no how, no way.

In my psychology and law class, we discovered that over 80 percent of the African American women who were asked if they thought O.J. Simpson was guilty responded, "No, a famous athlete like O.J. Simpson could not have done something like that. All-star football players couldn't do something that violent." They had already decided that Simpson was completely innocent because in their minds, famous athletes don't commit violent crimes. Hence, Marsha Clark was powerless. There was nothing that she could have done to get a guilty verdict. Nothing. Even if O.J .had confessed, it would have been probably been argued that it was coerced, and that would have led to unprecedented riots in Los Angeles.

So, how could God allow O.J. Simpson to get away with murder? What was the gift behind the appearance of injustice? Maybe God was trying to get our attention about the fact that we are still racially divided in the 1990s. Maybe God was trying to get our attention about the fact that domestic violence is still a huge problem in America today. Maybe God was trying to get our attention about all of the injustices that have been committed against African Americans throughout history in the U.S. What is it going to take for us to get that there is only ONE race—the human race—and that we are all ONE? When are we going to stop all of the hate crimes?

Why did the events at Columbine, Colorado, have to happen? How could three intelligent teenage boys kill their classmates with such violence? How could this happen in affluent, white America? Because white, affluent America needs to stop pointing the finger at Blacks, Hispanics, liberals, gays, poverty, drugs, alcohol and Jews. In my opinion, the purpose of the events at Columbine was to wake up affluent white America. God was saying that white, affluent America needs to take a long, hard look in the mirror and reevaluate what it is creating. This was the gift, or message, of Columbine.

The events at Columbine also happened because no one listened. No one took the time to listen to the three young men. They said that they were going to do this. They videotaped what they were going to do, but somewhere along the way we became too busy, too much in denial, to take the time to hear them. Here is another example of the gift behind a truly traumatic event—the importance of listening.

How could God allow Princess Diana to die in the prime of her life? How could God let such an important humanitarian die so abruptly? The miracle behind Princess Diana's death was that, for the first time, the entire world united in compassion. Every country, race, and political regime was touched by her passing. Her death demonstrated that humanity everywhere can unite in compassion and express unconditional love. This was unprecedented. Do you see what a powerful gift of hope that she gave us through her death? At humanity's core is an ability to express compassion which transcends race, wealth and political power. Unity was the gift of Diana's traumatic death.

God works in mysterious ways. She is truly in all things. Have you noticed that people unite whenever there is a natural disaster unite? When there are droughts in the South, farmers from the Midwest send bails of hay. When there are earthquakes, communities unite in compassion. Natural or man-made disasters often bring out the best in humanity. Whatever the event, no matter how traumatic, look for the gift. Always ask, "What is the gift behind this? What am I supposed to learn?" Always see the greater outcome. And so it is.

Chapter Eleven

The Imprint of Violence

Do you realize that the same people in Hollywood who say that video games do not influence violence will spend $1,000,000 for a 30 second spot during the Super Bowl? Why? To get you to buy their products. Do you realize that the military, various militia groups, the CIA and FBI use these same video games to train people to kill without emotion or remorse? (The above paragraph was paraphrased from Friendship with God by Neale Donald Walsch.) Are you aware that the highest number of violent acts committed against women occur during the Super Bowl? Men drink, their aggressions are aroused, and they react with violence when their team doesn't win.

In my opinion, Charleston Heston, spokesperson of the National Rifle Association, needs a reality check. (The NRA also needs a reality check.) Members of this organization are stuck in a past that no longer serves us. The 1950s are over, so get over it.

The Constitution of the United States was written over 200 years ago. Two hundred years ago, there were no AK-47's, no crack cocaine, no gang warfare, no automatic Uzis, no sawed-off shot guns, and no "cop killer" bullets. Two hundred years ago, we did not have a society that spent millions of dollars on the promotion of violence. The right to bear arms does not equal the right to bear assault weapons. Two hundred years ago, there were no Sony Play stations or Nintendos that programmed children's minds to believe that killing is just a game. A child who plays violent games on Nintendo for a few hours a day can become desensitized to violence. America in general has become desensitized to violence, far too desensitized, in my opinion. Each and every year movies, video games, and TV programs become more and more violent.

People, get involved in your children's life. Tell them they are wanted. Let them know that if others reject them or make fun of them, that doesn't make them BAD, WRONG, or NOT WANTED. Those who reject or tease others are so insecure that they need to make others feel bad, so they can feel good about themselves. Teenagers often feel that they have no identity or sense of purpose. Social Psychologist Milton Erikson wrote, "A teen will take on the identity of being 'bad' because to them, having a 'bad' identity is better than having no identity at all." If you give your children a sense of purpose and a sense that what they do and who they are is important, they WILL NOT turn to sex, drugs, or violence. If you don't know how to express love, GET HELP. Believe me, I know.

I became a bad boy by the time I was 14. I smoked pot every day during my junior year in high school. I "died" at the age of 16 from alcohol poisoning. Then, when I was 19, I stopped taking all drugs. I have no explanation for this. I just woke up one morning and said, "This is it, no more." I haven't done drugs in over 11 years. THANK YOU GOD!

I am not making pot-smoking wrong. In fact, I wish that they would make it legal. It could be a new source of paper, textiles, and rope. It is strong, durable and biodegradable. You can engineer it without THC. There is not a single case in which a person has ever overdosed or died from smoking pot. Legalizing pot and using it as a source of paper would eliminate the destruction of the Amazon rain forest, and it could be taxed to eliminate our national debt. In fact, this is probably why it is still illegal. Our national debt is a huge business for foreign bankers. Every penny you pay in income taxes goes to pay the interest on the national debt which is owned by foreign investors. (Don't even get me started on the IRS, a.k.a. Ignorance Related Slavery.)

In my opinion, marijuana has never led to violence. However, alcohol, a legal substance, is probably the number one cause of all domestic violence in the United States.

Chapter Twelve

Healing the Matrix of Race

I think that in order for African Americans to be fully acknowledged in our society, the leaders of this nation need extend to them a long overdue apology. Then, African Americans will need to forgive their forefathers for selling members of their own race into slavery. Additionally, I think that the leaders of this nation need to extend a long overdue apology to all Hispanics, Asians, Native Americans and women. I was discussing this issue with a friend of mine earlier today, and what follows is a result of that conversation. I think is very insightful and hope you will find it valuable.

I look at all of these religious groups who complain about "gangsta rap," and those who feel that it should be banned. They claim that it only leads to violence and irrational behavior, such as teen pregnancy and illicit drug usage. I want to look at these leaders and say, "Well, duh…" If you suppress the civil rights of a race of humans—namely, African Americans—for generations, the oppressed will eventually experience feelings of hostility towards the oppressors. This hostility towards the white race has now expressed itself in gangsta rap. I am not condoning or endorsing gangsta rap. I am just pointing out that if you suppress a race of individuals long enough, they will respond with hostility.

This is why hate groups like the KKK are growing at an alarming rate. They get to point the finger at gangsta rap without acknowledging the real cause of it. They use emotional appeals and say, "Listen to what they are saying about us white folks. If we don't put a stop to this now, they are going to kill all of us. Just listen to the lyrics of this rap music." Fear feeds into fear. If you are broke and starving, it becomes easy to blame the other race. Hate groups and cults alike target people with social problems. People with social problems often blame society for their ill-fated condition.

If another race is perceived as a threat to a person's already bleak condition, whether real or imaginary, then that race becomes the sole cause. I laugh at the idea that Mexican immigrants are taking away American jobs. I live in La Mesa, New Mexico, which is about 35 miles north of Juarez, Mexico. This is a small agricultural community with a base of immigrant farm workers. For one week last year, I worked in the fields along with the immigrants. The days were long and the sun unbearable. I seriously doubt that most American men would willingly do this work for less than $4 or $5 an hour. I can assure American wage earners that these immigrants are not taking jobs considered desirable by today's standards. The perceived threat of Mexican immigrants stealing jobs is just that. It is perceived without any truth behind it. It is based on an emotional appeals that says, "Mexicans are stealing your jobs and that is why you can't pay your bills." This is exactly how Adolf Hitler convinced his nation to kill 6 million Jews during WWII. He blamed the economic hardships of Germany on the Jews. This has nothing to do with the truth. In fact, most social threats are created out of fear. They are imagined.

This is also how cults attract followers: "You have problems in your life because of them, and I have the solution." The solution, of course, involves giving everything to the cult leaders, which leaves you more penniless than before. But that is okay because by giving everything to God, all of your problems are going to be solved. Most cults take away your possessions and have you fast for a few days after joining them. This deprivation reduces your capacity to think logically and you become like a zombie, open to whatever the cult leader tells you. You then become a recruiter. Now, not only are you a member of the cult, but you are also a recruiter. You have an identity, a sense of purpose and a deep sense of belonging. This is why you feel so high—not because you have found the truth, but because you have an identity. Your previous identity didn't work or was rejected by your peers. Now you have a new identity and are accepted by those who are of like mind. This creates a powerful matrix of consciousness .Of course you feel that you have found God. How else could Hitler have convinced a handful of people to commit such atrocities against another race? When Germany experienced economic hardship, the people of the German race lost their identities. There is no greater pain than losing sense of oneself.

Cults and hate groups operate in an identical manner. Their imprints of lost identities, combined with an imagined racial threat to their survival, creates a powerful matrix of blame and hatred towards the "out group." Combine this matrix of hatred and blame with the imprint of suppression and oppression inherit in the matrix of the African American race, and you can begin to understand why we have racial problems in America today. Matrixes seek each other out. This is the law of attraction unfolding here. This is what we must heal. We must begin to see that there is only one race—the human race.

I have been following the recent debate over the confederate flag in South Carolina. When I lived in Charleston, I could not believe how a city with such grace, beauty, elegance and charm could allow the KKK to openly march down historic King St. In my opinion, the Confederate flag is not a symbol of heritage. The glory of the red, white and blue—now that is heritage. In my opinion, the Confederate flag represents separation, division, war, and hatred. The South lost, GET OVER IT! As I stated earlier, these hate groups state that God's only son was white. Therefore, the white race is superior. However, Jesus was not God's only son and he couldn't have been white. Two thousand years ago in the Middle East, there were no Caucasians. None, period! Jesus would have had an olive complexion. He would have been one of those "fucking" Arabs.

Despite the hardships placed on African Americans, they must realize that other races have been equally suppressed throughout history. In my opinion, the Native Americans have faced the greatest hardship on the face of this Earth. I also believe that we have completely ignored the fact that women and children are suppressed, but in more subtle ways. Women continue to suffer great hardships in America.

Chapter Thirteen

Healing the Matrix of Gender

The first thing we need to do to heal the battle of the sexes is to end the practice of paying women 69 cents for every dollar that a man earns for the same job. Second, we need to stop making being "different" wrong. It is perfectly alright that men do certain things better than women, and that women do certain things better than men.

In our strive for equality, we have become more separate. Men and women struggle so much because men want women to think the way men do, and women want men to think the way women do. We must realize that men and women think differently from each other. We need to recognize that these differences don't make the opposite sex unequal. I think we need to redefine the position that being different means being unequal. We often view what is different from ourselves as a threat to our survival. We follow outdated role models that remain in conflict with each other.

I have often said that the issue of abortion keeps women divided. As long as women remain divided, they will remain suppressed in today's political and corporate realms. Women have forgotten that they have a right to not bear children. I think that women would have a strong voice in a man's world if they could say, "I am personally against abortion. However, it is in the best interest of all to keep abortion safe and legal." It is interesting to note that in areas where the religious right have deemed abortions immoral, and where abortions are not tolerated, crime is 80 percent higher than the national average. In areas where abortions are considered an option and that option is exercised, crime is below the national average.

What is the correlation here? Well, I believe that the emotional state of the mother and father during pregnancy has a direct bearing on the matrix of a child. If an unborn child's parents want to abort and the morals of their environment won't allow it, those feelings of not being wanted become imprinted in the child's matrix. In my opinion, there is no greater wound than feeling unwanted. This feeling condemns a person to believing she is bad. This core belief, "I am bad," in my opinion, leads to all crime.

Women did not come to Earth for the sole purpose of creating children. Women have minds, emotions and souls that are longing to be listened to. Most importantly, they are not objects. Relationships and marriage are not about ownership. Your wife is not something you purchased at the electronic store; she did not come with a receipt. I think we need to re-write the "Book of Genesis" and stop blaming Eve for tempting Adam to eat the forbidden fruit. We need to honor women, to recognize and honor the divine feminine within us all. I think we need to integrate the masculine and feminine within us. As we begin to balance the male and female within, we will no longer view the opposite sex as different, but rather an aspect of the whole self. As we become integrated, we will learn to embrace all different aspects of self. We will cease to define being different as wrong, bad, or inadequate. We will heal. Can you imagine what the world would be like if men had to bear children? Do you think that condoms and birth control devices would be more acceptable? Do you think we would promote this idea of mass procreation? Probably not, I would guess, but this is something to think about.

Chapter Fourteen

The Matrix of Dr. Deeper

When I was training to be a hypnotherapist through the National Guild of Hypnotists *http://www.NGH.net*, I was nicknamed "Dr. Deeper." This was due to my ability to place difficult subjects into a very deep state, and to the way that I pronounced the word "deeper" in my inductions. ("Deeeepeeerrrrrr.")

A couple of years passed, and due to my endowment and good looks, Dr. Deeper began to include a few sexual innuendoes. Dr. Deeper became a facade of security behind which I could hide my deep-seated feelings of guilt, shame and inadequacies. My playboy persona was a tool I used to numb my feelings of insecurity. My alter ego, Dr. Deeper, became irresponsible, reckless, manipulative, lazy and uncaring. I developed so much blame, rage, and anger towards society that I went into withdrawal. Escaping on the Internet became a drug I used to avoid daily obligations and responsibilities. I developed an attitude that "the world owes me," and I was going to make sure that everyone was going to pay their dues to me, the great walk-in from the future.

As an only child, I had learned that if I was in trouble, there would always be someone to bail me out. Usually it was my grandmother. I never had to be responsible for myself. My mother and father divorced when I was around 3 years old. Shortly after that, I would stand in the living room and ask my mom, "When is daddy coming home?" She would just stare at me in her own numbness and say nothing. Nothing. I now believe that at that moment, I decided that I was bad and that I was the sole cause of my parent's divorce. The imprint of that decision led to pot smoking, alcohol overdose, depression, and more recently, the persona of Dr. Deeper. I learned to matter most when I was being, the bad boy. I received the most attention when I played the bad boy role.

The Internet enabled me to contact numerous women. I sent them pictures of my endowment as a way to receive sexual attention. Although there were a lot of contacts, I only had sexual relations with two women from the net. Dr. Deeper was my fantasy of being Don Juan, a real womanizer. So, I have slept with 10 women. Two of them were married and yes, I have done the Bill and Monica thing with another married woman. I have been contacted by a couple of men who are interested in oral sex.

So, this is my skeleton closet. Dr. Deeper felt secure and confident. Mark Patterson, on the other hand, experienced deep feelings of fear, guilt, shame and inadequacies. Dr. Deeper set out on a path to prove that Mark was not a failure as a male—a very destructive path, which I was changed once I became aware of my personal lie.

During the past few years, I repeatedly dreamt that I was in my late 20s and still living at home. I became aware of these dreams and as I began to dream, I would think to myself, *I am 29 years old and I haven't lived at home in 10 years, what am I still doing here?* I called up my friend, Dr. Kelley Elkins, and asked him about these dreams

"We have found that emotionally speaking, 95 percent of our clients are still living at home waiting for someone to take care of them, or they are waiting to be told what to do," said Elkins.

His partner, Toni Delgado, added, "We are all still in diapers." I thought to myself, *emotionally stuck still at home*. Toni then suggested that I take time to discover my personal lie. When she said the words "personal lie," I was terrified to the bone. Uncovering my personal lie would be one of the most difficult challenges I could possibly face. I knew that if I confronted my lie, I would have to give up the facade that said: "I am not capable." "I am bad and unworthy." However, I also knew that if something terrified me, I had to confront it.

The following weekend, I spent three hours with Toni and discovered what my core beliefs about myself actually were. (If you don't know what your core beliefs about yourself are, you need to find out, as they literally control every aspect of your life.) As we came to the end of the session, she said, "In order for this to be true, you must feel that you are not wanted and not understood. No matter what you do, it won't make a difference anyway, so you stop trying."

A flood of tears squirted from my eyes upon reaching my personal lie. I must have cried for over 30 minutes. The key here is just that—it is a lie, not the truth. For whatever reason, my ego had ignored my ability to go within the magical closet, and instead turned to others to solve problems. If you find yourself always looking for others to bail you out, you need to decide that you are capable of solving the problem yourself. If your life is not working, you have been given the opportunity to realize that you are capable of creating the life that you want to live. This imprint of being bad, of not being capable, has probably caused more problems in my life than anything else.

A few years ago, I found myself in a very crazy relationship. Every few months, either on campus, in a classroom, or at the mall, a Hispanic female kept popping into my life. In all honesty, she looked more like a "hoochie mama" than someone I would consider going out with. For whatever reason, she would always tell me how handsome I was, touch me, and become all giggles when she talked to me. I couldn't figure out why this woman kept appearing in my life.

One day, I ran into her at a local restaurant and she asked me if I would like to go out with her and her children. Reluctantly I agreed, and ended up going to the mall with her and her three kids. I found out that she had suffered a lot of abuse in her life. She had been abused by her mother, raped by her grandfather at the age of 14, and beaten and nearly killed by her second husband, who pushed her off a 14-foot bridge.

I tend to draw abused women into my life. It seems that no matter how hurt or abused they have been, I have a way of opening their hearts to love once again. Maybe this is my gift, maybe it is my curse. She called me the following week, and I soon discovered that she really wasn't a hoochie mama. For whatever reason, she just dressed that way. She was extremely self-conscious about her body and had only had experienced sex with a few men. (There was nothing wrong with her body—34DD-24-34—and her appearance reminded me of Marilyn Monroe.) She was painfully self-aware.

As we continued to go out, I became aware of how much pain she was in. Her house was always a mess. Her clothes were piled everywhere, and toys were two and three feet high in the kids' rooms. She hooked into the matrix of Dr. Deeper, who was also a superman type: "I can do anything. I am here to save you and I am here to fix you. You need to be saved." I was convinced that if she would listen to me and let me help her, the relationship would get better. She would get better. I could would make it work. Yes, I had all of the answers. So, I spent numerous hours helping her clean her house, picking up clothes, toys, and video games, and providing some structure for her kids. One afternoon, we did 25 to 30 loads of laundry to get caught up.

As we continued with our relationship, she told me that she smoked "crack" cocaine. She had a really strange addiction. I don't know a lot about crack cocaine, but it seems that people who use it smoke it constantly—it is that addictive. She, however, was a binge smoker. She would get completely high, out of her mind, and then not do it again for four months. (I can be really naive, so this may not be possible.) She called me Christmas night—out of her mind and barely coherent—and said that she was on crack. I was in Iowa at the time and she was in New Mexico. If I had been in New Mexico, I probably would have ended the relationship right there. But again, Dr. Deeper said, "I didn't do enough. I didn't love her enough. I can save her. I shouldn't have gone home for Christmas, I should have stayed with her. I didn't do enough." She really pushed my buttons.

I remember spending $700 during one week on her and her kids, and a few days later spending another $400 to have her car fixed. Despite all of this, she looked at me one day and said, "You couldn't possibly provide for the needs of me and my family." For whatever reason, I allowed her to make me feel inadequate and guilty as a male. Again, this is how the imprints within our matrix attract imprints within the matrix of others. I stayed in the relationship, determined to prove to her that I was enough.

As we continued our dance, I became aware of how much she reflected my deepest wounds. She was like my shadow self in physical form. She always compared herself to how she used to be before her accident. I always compared myself to how happy I used to be when I lived in Charleston, South Carolina. (As long as you constantly compare yourself to the past, you will remain miserable.) She held on to a deep feeling that she was guilty of allowing herself to be sexually violated. I, too, held deep feelings of guilt for the same reason. She was a perfect mirror for all of my issues around not being enough. She constantly looked at herself in the mirror, as she was overly-self conscious. I, too, at times, am painfully self-conscious. Often, she would take off and not deal with obligations and responsibilities. I, too, am a master at this game of avoidance. She was the only person I ever met who could spend money faster than I could.

Yet, this is what we do in our relationships. We "energetically loop" with those who reflect back to us our own unresolved issues. Your life is perfect just the way that it is because it is a mirror of how you flow your energy. God doesn't answer your prayers, She responds, or answers, to your vibration. So, if you ask God for a new, healthy relationship, yet at a core level believe you are unlovable, that what you are vibrating. Thus, God answers your vibration. God responds to your belief that you are unlovable. Due to the law of attraction, you will attract a mate who will tell you exactly how unlovable you are. You will then hate everyone of the opposite sex, label them as jerks, and despise God in the process.

Soon, I began to realize that I was carrying all of my girlfriend's blame, rage, and anger. I went from having one glass of wine a week to having two to three beers a day. I was allowing my relationship with her to destroy me. Late one evening, her 5-year-old daughter was screaming and crying. No matter what we tried to do, she wouldn't stop. Finally, I lost it. I picked her up and shook her. I really shook her. This was about 2 a.m. I set her down, went into the den and cried. I had always sworn that I would never do something like that, but I did. At that moment, I knew it was over. I had to leave the relationship. Around 6 a.m., I woke up and wrote her a note, telling her it was over. She always said that I couldn't handle the kids. The truth was that I couldn't handle her. I got up and left. I am thankful for that relationship. It was a mirror of the stuff I didn't want to look at. She was perhaps my greatest teacher. I hope that someday she will see that I was one of hers.

Chapter Fifteen

The Matrix of Las Cruces, New Mexico

(Las Clueless, that it is.) I have heard numerous people in the New Age community say, that they are here on Earth to resolve their fears. Well, if you are serious about resolving your fears, then get your ass down here to the desert. The metaphor of the desert is that there is no where to hide. It is barren and you are completely exposed. You certainly cannot hide from yourself.

The desert is very grounding. Most of us want nothing to do with our bodies; we would just as soon leave them as be in them. When we are not grounded, we make poor decisions that are not based in this reality. The desert places you in your body. It creates mirages and reflects all of your fears back to you. Las Cruces is a wonderful place to become stripped of your identity and everything else, until you become aware of who you really are. The desert brings all of your unresolved issues to the surface.

The Apache Indians once lived in this part of the country, and it is said that they were the toughest of the Native Peoples. This is a place where people with strength, character, endurance and faith survive. Numerous New Agers have come and gone, as it is very intense here. Most of them last about six months and decide that they can't handle what the desert reflects back to them. I have tried to run away from Las Cruces many times. The first year, I was convinced that moving back to Charleston would solve all of my problems. But I kept getting messages that I was in the right place at the right time and that all was well. Despite the struggle, deprivation and frustration, I knew that I was supposed to be here.

Within six months of moving here, I was told that people are sent to Las Cruces to resolve their fears. It has also been said that Las Cruces is where all of the great masters have gathered for the last stand. This is the city of the crosses, where you place your sins on the cross and pray that you can resurrect and transcend them. So, if you want to meet your shadow and all of the mirages that it can and will create for you, I personally invite you to come to Las Cruces, New Mexico. Here you will become grounded, lose your identity, and become aware of who you really are.

Chapter Sixteen

The Matrix of Sound

From the Tibetan monks, to the mystery schools of Egypt, to Jewish mysticism—it has been said that all creation begins with sound: "In the beginning was the word." In the beginning was a sound—a wave form—that was responsible for all creation.

There is no greater tool for healing, transformation, and self-empowerment than the spoken word. Your voice is one of the greatest gifts that God gave you. The sound of your voice reflects who you are and where you are at in any given moment. Your voice resonates your inner power. When you tell a lie, does your voice crack? Do you cover your mouth when you are being dishonest with someone? You can tell a person's frame of mind by the sound of his voice. If you take the time to meditate and do deep breathing, you will notice that your voice deepens, reflecting that you are more connected to your inner being. You can know everything about a person's state of mind by the voice. Have you ever noticed a person's laugher? Is it full and robust or does it drive you crazy? Your ability to create your life is done through the spoken word. Former President Ronald Reagan said over and over again, "I can't recall." Now, he really can't recall.

The word "enchantment" implies "to become one with God by chanting." In my opinion there is no more powerful tool for enlightenment then toning. If you look at all of the masters' names, you will find that they have something in common: Budd(ah), Yoganad(a), Sia Bab(a), Mer

112 • You Are God

Bab(a), Yashew(a), and Krishin(a). They all have the "ah" sound, the vibration of creation. When chanting "Ahhhhhh," you are setting into motion a powerful vibration that enables you to manifest your heart's desires. "Ahhhhhh" invokes the creation process. "Ohmmm," on the other hand, is the sound of God's vibration. "Ohmmm" enables you to create a deeper connection to your own soul, and thus connect to God. Based on my own experience, it is best to connect inwardly with the sound of the "Ohmmm," and then create with "Ahhhhhh." You will probably find it difficult to do either one of these unless you have an open heart.

One of the most powerful processes for opening the heart on all levels involves using the sound of the owl: "Hooooo." This amazing sound will open your heart to the angelic realms. "Hooooo." Your vibration will fly and you will be tapped in, tuned in, turned on and ready to manifest your heart's desires.

Here are the keys to manifesting with sound. First, state your intention: "It is my intention to use this sound to open my heart to the divine and angelic realms." Second, use the "Hooooo" sound to open your heart and center your mind. Tone the "Hooooo" sound for about 10 to 15 minutes. Next, state your desired manifestations in the following way: "I am thankful for receiving $10,000. 'Ahhhhhh.' I am thankful for being in the right relationship. 'Ahhhhhh.' I am thankful for being a successful _____. 'Ahhhhhh.' I am thankful for being healed. 'Ahhhhhh.'" Do as many of these as you want; the possibilities are endless. What is important here is that you are expressing thanks for already having it. The sound of "Ahhhhhh" sets it into creation. Finally, spend 10 to 15 minutes doing "Ohmmm." This completes the creation process and enables you to honor your inner Christ, the God self, who you really are. I know that this process works. Use this great gift from God and it will create miracles in your life. (Special thanks to Dr. Wayne Dyer for the information in this chapter.)

Chapter Seventeen

The Matrix of the Imagination

In the "Book of Genesis," God states that man was created in "His" image and likeness. What does this mean, that man was created in God's image and likeness? Let's assume that it is actually possible to describe God. What words would you use? "Unlimited," "creative," "boundless" and "powerful" could be just a few. Now, how would you describe the quality of imagination? "Unlimited," "creative," "boundless" and "powerful"... hmmmm...there seem to be some similarities here. How interesting.

I believe that our ability to imagine is what makes us Gods. Other species may communicate, think, cry, and procreate, but the imagination is unique to us. Our ability to imagine enables us to create, and when we learn to focus our imagination towards a certain goal over a period of time, we will create that goal. However, we tend to divert our energies into far too many aspects of our lives. How many times do we start 10 projects, only to finish three of them? Or how many times do we over-extend ourselves until we burn out.

The only difference between you and a genius is that the genius is able to focus there attention in one area for a long period of time. When Einstein developed his theory of relativity, he used his imagination. He imagined what it would be like to be a particle or a wave form of light. As he continued to play with his imagination, he became aware that the imagination of light itself was a stream of consciousness. As he tuned into that stream of consciousness, he developed the theory of relativity.

As you use your imagination, you begin to develop parts of your brain that have been asleep since you were a child. When you awaken the imagination, you are awakening the matrix of God within. You are never closer to God then you are right here, right now, in the physical. You cannot experience God when you leave your physical body. Without a body, you cannot imagine, achieve orgasm, create, or transform the non-physical into the physical. Your ability to be a creator depends on your physical existence. That is why it is said that the greatest temple of God, the most holy and sacred, is your body. This, my dear friends, is God's greatest gift to you: the ability to transform the non-physical into the physical. As you learn to master your imagination and focus it towards a desired goal, you will have learned to master your thoughts. This is why you are here. You have been sent to the physical from the non-physical to demonstrate your KNOWING. Jesus represented the "possible human" because he demonstrated his KNOWING. He was a master of his own thoughts and he manifested God on Earth.

Chapter Eighteen

The Matrix of the Possible Human

As Keanau Reeves released his limitations of what he thought was possible in the movie "The Matrix," he began to create anything he could imagine. He became God. I have walked on 2,000 degree coals and did not burn my feet. (Phosphorous coals were not used, and I can assure you that the coals were extremely hot.) Fire-walking is a very important and effective way to over come limiting core beliefs. I hope someday to walk on water. (Of course, walking on water is a metaphor for demonstrating control over your emotional fears. I feel that people will eventually be able to walk on water.) When we master our emotions—controlling them without suppressing them—we become masters of our lives.

Since my NDE, I have dreamed about moving objects with my mind, placing my hand through a wall and levitating. More recently I dreamed that I resurrected 15 dead people simultaneously. This dream took place about 10-15 years in the future, and I had become like Jesus. The amount of peace and love that I felt was overwhelming. God's love—the feeling of peace and joy—is here for us right now if we are willing to accept it, believe it, and proclaim that it is ours to have. When you experience something like that, you realize that everything we worry about is trivial, a joke compared to the matrix of unconditional love your soul longs you to tune into. As we have fragmented our connection to God, our light bodies— our life force—has diminished into nothingness. This is why the mystics of India and the Yogis in Central America call us the walking dead. We are completely unconscious.

If you don't think that we are walking zombies, stand outside of Walmart and watch people walk into the store. We are all on auto-pilot, which is scary. We aren't aware of our thoughts, motives, or actions, yet we are in continual reaction. We are not even aware of our own breath, yet breath connects us to the life force. When we are under stress and shut down, we don't allow breathing to do its job and return us to a state of oneness. Negative emotions, fear, and being someone we are not rob us of our life force. When we feel guilty, our being is in guilt and we become guilt. When we are resentful, our being is in resentment and we become it. When we are angry, our being is in anger and we become angry. When we say yes to other people when we want to say no and resent ourselves in turn, we rob our life force. When we lie to others and ourselves, we rob our life force.

We spend 90 percent of our time being who we are not in order to survive. This is not love. This is fear—of rejection, abandonment, and of disappointing others—that is driving our lives, not love. Yet, love is our natural state. This is sin, missing the mark of your inner being, which is love, God, Christ. When your inner being is in love, you become love. You become one with God; you become God. Your matrix becomes the natural self. As you become the love that you are, you will become the "possible hu-man," the divine being you are.

Chapter Nineteen

The Matrix of the Future

One morning, you will wake up and realize it has all been a dream. You will see how connected you are to all life. You will know why you created and experienced all of the drama in your life, and will realize it was a variety of plays that you created for yourself. You will understand that you are the director, playwright, editor and star. You will see yourself in all things, people, and places. You will know why you chose the parents that you did. You will understand why you ate all the junk food, and how it kept you from being one with God. You will understand how you have used weight, illness, disease and depression as ways to protect you from others. These things became your security blanket to protect you from becoming too close to anyone. It will not matter whether there is a one-world order or not, because you will learn how to create from within. It will not matter if the oceans rise 100 feet, because you will say, "Go here" and you will be taken to safety. It will not matter if the sun doesn't shine for three days, for you will know the presence of your own soul. It will not matter what the future brings because you will be fully present in the moment.

I was sent from the future to alter the past, so that your "now" can be a beautiful experience. I am not the only one; there are many "strangers" among us. Most of your doomsday prophecies have not happened, correct? Yet the Hopi Indians still claim in the Hopi Prophecy, "Yes, it said, that in the winter of 1998, there would be world purification day." They seem to ignore the fact that the prediction was wrong, and continue to proclaim that the Hopi Prophecy is the truth. The Hopis have become as self-righteous as the fundamentalists. Be careful, or you will become what you hate.

My soul and others spend countless nights working with the leaders of the world and their inner beings in the matrix of the dreams. As far as we can tell, they seem to be listening. Not at the pace we would like, but they are listening. We love this planet too much to allow Gaia to be destroyed. So, what is going to happen in the future?

For those of you who are 'rassling fans, it is interesting to note the story line created by Ted Turner's Atlanta-based World Championship Wrestling (WCW) during the past two years. The WCW became divided by a group of wrestlers known as the New World Order (NWO). After a couple of years of chaos, the NWO broke into two separate factions and eventually collapsed. Do you think that a person who donates $1 billion to the UN might have some insight into the near future? Imagine that...

In the future, cancer and AIDS will be cured by using light, color and sound. Someone will finally figure out that the frequency used by dolphins and whales to communicate is the vibration of unconditional love. This frequency, or sound wave, will become replicated as a means to cure most incurable illnesses. Unfortunately, the U.S. Naval department thinks it is cool to blast sound waves under water. These sound waves are disrupting the most highly evolved species on this planet.

Alternative healing will no longer be alternative, but will become mainstream. Past life therapy will become the most sought-after tool for self-empowerment.

More communities will be based on spirituality and communal living. There will be more marriages or partnerships involving two or more individuals, and gay marriages will be more open and commonplace.

Intuitive abilities will increase, as will communications with angels and other life forms.

The Internet will bring an end to big business in Washington, D.C.

A nuclear reaction might occur in the United States. If this happens, a green party movement candidate will become president of the United States. Around 2,008, the president of the United States will be a walk-in.

Science and religion will be bridged into one. You may want to pay attention to a man by the name of David Hudson. He will play an important role in this change.

The biggest threat to world peace is the potential conflict between North and South Korea. The situation is so terrible that North Koreans are eating their children to survive. Japan and China will struggle to gain control of Korea.

China will become a democracy, signaling the time of Armageddon Two events will occur—one in China and one in Israel. A third world war will seem to be inevitable but miraculously, a solution will be found and war will be avoided. The individual who brings about the solution will be the modern Christ. On the other side of the scale is the anti-Christ, an individual living in Turkey. I don't think that we need these individuals, but we have created so many thought forms around this event that we have brought them into our matrix of reality.

India and Pakistan must work to resolve their conflicts or they may go to war—nuclear war—against each other. I think this can be avoided.

Everything needed for a One World Government is in place. Individuals involved are waiting for the stock market to crash in the U.S. If it does, it will not last long.

If the Soviet Union returns to a communist form of government, it will be short lived. Once people taste freedom, they will not let go of it very easily.

It is possible that the U.S. will return to the gold standard and that all credit debt will be expunged. You will see more of bartering economies in the U.S.

Free energy devices will become more common, and electric trains will take over the mass transit system. People will worry about the ozone layer becoming more and more depleted, so an effort to reduce the number of cars and fossil fuels will be enforced.

However, all consciousness is determined by light. As the frequency of light changes, the levels of consciousness also change on a given planet. As the ozone layer is depleted, a new light will be introduced to this planet which has the potential to shift its consciousness. Eventually, the Earth will move to another matrix and become part of a binary solar system. That Earth is there waiting for us. We will realize that we have been told a history that is not very accurate. All of the truths are coming out. There will be no more secrets, no more cover-ups or scandals. Extraterrestrial will become your next door neighbors. Those in power will fall and the meek shall inherit the Earth.

There will be individuals on this planet who will be able to look into the eyes of another and read the DNA coding contained within the eye. They will know everything about that person and how to direct her towards her goals. These people are holographic readers who understand the hologram within the eye. They are counselors from the planet Sirius who have been sent here to help individuals during the transition time. We will soon realize that evidence of extraterrestrial life has been on Earth all along. We will soon realize that we are not alone. Most importantly, we will remember our connection to God and peace will prevail on Earth.

This transition can be a very beautiful one, if you are willing to allow it to be so. There is always a way out, and the way out is through you. Pay attention to the children, for they will take us back home to God. No matter how out of control they appear, they will lead the way. Love and nurture them. Take their hand and let them lead you to God.

The future is listening. Heaven on Earth is right here, right now. If you can allow your heart to open to love and let your children become your greatest teachers, Heaven will appear right before your eyes and you won't have to leave your body behind. Ascension is at hand and this time no one, no one, will be left behind. You are loved beyond belief. You are the light and the way. You are the Christ. You are the messenger. You are God's child with whom She is most pleased. Go, be at peace and do your best.

About the Author

Mark Clinton Patterson holds a BA in Psychology from NMSU in Las Cruces, NM. On February 1st, 1986 he had an NDE. This experience gave him a greater insight into our purpose from being here. He hopes that these truths will lead others into Self-Mastery. Mark is a walk-in.

References

Dr. Kelley Elkins DC and Toni Delgado "Personal Lie" Process work
Dr. Valerie Hunt, "Infinite Mind"
Dr. Jon Kaiser
Tom Kenyon's Garvandana "Chanting Praises to God"
Drunvalo Melchizedek, Flower of Life Seminar and the Mer-Ka-Ba meditation
Abraham Maslow's Hierarchy of Needs
Jerry and Ester Hicks and the teachings of Abraham
Dr. Wayne Dyer's Meditation for Manifesting
"The Matrix"
"Patch Adams"
John Bradshaw "Healing the Shame that Binds You & Homecoming"
WCW/N.W.O. Ted Turner's Wrestling Promotion

Bibliography

Brennan, Barbara Ann **Hands of Light** Bantam New Age. New York (1991)

Carroll, Lee **Kryon the Journey Home** Hay House. Carlsbad, California (1997)

Clark, Keith **You're Smart Enough to be Your Own Suergon**

Chopra, Deepak **Ageless Body Timeless Mind** Bantam New Age. New York (1993)

Forrest, Waves *AIDS as Biological and Psychological Warfare www.above-topsecret.com/aids.html* (1999)

Null, Gary *Power Profits and Politic of AIDS* Gary Null, (1997)

Page, Ken **The Way it Works** Ken Page Bastrop, Texas (1998)

Sutphen, Tara *"Abenda Channels"* **www.dicksutphen.com** 2000

Virtue, Doreen **The Light Worker's Way** Hay House. Carlsbad, California (1997)

Walsch, Neale Donald **Friendship with God** Putnam. New York (1999)

Walsch, Neale Donald **Conversations with God** Putnam New York (1993)

CPSIA information can be obtained at www.ICGtesting.com
Printed in the USA
LVOW130905231212

312967LV00001B/203/A